DATE DUE

Welfare Reform

The Politics
of
Wealth
and
Poverty

IDEAS in CONFLICT

Gary E. McCuen

publications inc.

411 Mallalieu Drive
Hudson, Wisconsin 54016
Phone (715) 386-7113

Illustration and Photo Credits

Bureau of the Census 131; Carol & Simpson 89; Congressional Reference Service 59, 65; Government Accounting Office 159; Heritage Foundation 33, 47, 71; Social Security Administration 137; Social Welfare History Archives, University of Minnesota 11, 53, 117; State Electronic Databases 125; *Star Tribune*, Minneapolis/St. Paul 15, 17, 23.

publications inc.

© 1996 by Gary E. McCuen Publications, Inc.
411 Mallalieu Drive, Hudson, Wisconsin 54016

(715) 386-7113

International Standard Book Number
0-86596-136-0
Printed in the United States of America

CONTENTS

Ideas in Conflict

Chapter 1   THE WELFARE POLICY DEBATE

Chapter 2   **CHILDREN, TEEN PREGNANCY AND
               THE DISABLED**

Chapter 3 CHARITY, CHURCH AND WELFARE

REASONING SKILL DEVELOPMENT

These activities may be used as individualized study guides for
students in libraries and resource centers or as discussion catalysts
in small group and classroom discussions.

IDEAS in CONFLICT

This series features ideas in conflict on political, social, and moral issues. It presents counterpoints, debates, opinions, commentary, and analysis for use in libraries and classrooms. Each title in the series uses one or more of the following basic elements:

Introductions that present an issue overview giving historic background and/or a description of the controversy.

Counterpoints and debates carefully chosen from publications, books, and position papers on the political right and left to help librarians and teachers respond to requests that treatment of public issues be fair and balanced.

Symposiums and forums that go beyond debates that can polarize and oversimplify. These present commentary from across the political spectrum that reflect how complex issues attract many shades of opinion.

A *global* emphasis with foreign perspectives and surveys on various moral questions and political issues that will help readers to place subject matter in a less culture-bound and ethnocentric frame of reference. In an ever-shrinking and interdependent world, understanding and cooperation are essential. Many issues are global in nature and can be effectively dealt with only by common efforts and international understanding.

Reasoning skill study guides and discussion activities provide ready-made tools for helping with critical reading and evaluation of content. The guides and activities deal with one or more of the following:

RECOGNIZING AUTHOR'S POINT OF VIEW

INTERPRETING EDITORIAL CARTOONS

VALUES IN CONFLICT

WHAT IS EDITORIAL BIAS?

WHAT IS SEX BIAS?

WHAT IS POLITICAL BIAS?

WHAT IS ETHNOCENTRIC BIAS?

WHAT IS RACE BIAS?

WHAT IS RELIGIOUS BIAS?

*From across **the political spectrum** varied sources are presented for research projects and classroom discussions. Diverse opinions in the series come from magazines, newspapers, syndicated columnists, books, political speeches, foreign nations, and position papers by corporations and nonprofit institutions.*

About the Editor

Gary E. McCuen is an editor and publisher of anthologies for libraries and discussion materials for schools and colleges. His publications have specialized in social, moral and political conflict. They include books, pamphlets, cassettes, tabloids, filmstrips and simulation games, most of them created from his many years of experience in teaching and educational publishing.

READING

1

HOW AMERICA CARES FOR ITS POOR

- Historical Overview
- Federal Assistance: Is Everyone on the Dole?
- Defining Corporate Welfare

Jean Hopfensperger

Jean Hopfensperger is a staff writer at the Star Tribune, *Minneapolis- St. Paul. In the following piece, she interviewed Clarke Chambers, Professor Emeritus at the University of Minnesota. Chambers has published many materials on the history of welfare and founded the Social Welfare Archives at the University of Minnesota. The second part of the overview is devoted to how federal assistance is divided among different economic classes in American society. The third part is about corporate tax breaks and subsidies, what many refer to as corporate welfare.*

■ **POINTS TO CONSIDER**

1. Discuss the traditional community role in public assistance through the 1930s.

2. What were some of the earliest welfare reforms and why were they made?

3. Describe the welfare institutions of the 19th century.

4. Explain the 19th century distinction between "deserving" and "undeserving" poor. How did those who largely remained outside the welfare system, such as immigrants, care for their poor?

5. Discuss Chambers' statement that there is a "continuity" in American welfare discourse. What are some of the continuous principles and anxieties of Americans regarding public assistance?

HISTORICAL OVERVIEW[1]

When Clarke Chambers hears clamoring for welfare reform from Washington, the ideas sound very familiar. Rehabilitate the poor. Build orphanages. Give states more responsibility for the poor. Get charities more involved. Many of these ideas have been around since colonial America, says the nationally known scholar on the history of social welfare.

Until the Social Security Act of 1935, it was local governments, private charities, family and friends who took care of the poor. The birth of Aid to Families with Dependent Children, Social Security and other entitlement programs was the first time the federal government got in the business of running a program to finance the needy, he said.

Chambers, a Professor Emeritus at the University of Minnesota, has published dozens of articles and books on the history of welfare in America over the past 30 years. He also founded the Social Welfare Archives at the University, a national repository of books, pamphlets and information on the nation's earliest social welfare programs.

Q Welfare is the subject of enormous debate today. How did this country care for poor people before we had this thing called welfare? And who received it?

A Starting in the colonial period, there was a commitment at the local level to provide assistance to those who were really in need. And the populations in need pretty well reflect the populations that are in need in the 19th through the 20th century...families left stranded by death, or illness, aged persons, persons who suffered various kinds of disabilities. And it was local government — the township, the county — that provided, out of property taxes, funds for the assistance.

Q What did they do for these people?

A Two things. They gave modest grants to persons in their own homes to see them through these times. A mother, for example, might be left with three children after her husband died of malaria. If she were competent, that is if she were healthy and reasonably sane, the revenue went to her and she took care of

[1]Jean Hopfensperger, "How Has America Cared for Its Poor?," **Star Tribune**, January 13, 1995. Reprinted with permission from the **Star Tribune**, Minneapolis-St. Paul.

the family until she was remarried or made other arrangements.

However, in the case with older persons who had become incapacitated by age and illness, frequently there was a foster-age arrangement. They would be placed in the home of someone else, who would then receive a modest stipend for caring for that person until he or she died...As for children, with full orphans, these children were "placed out," as the saying went. If they were infants or very young, there would be a stipend for the host family. And if they were older, that is six, seven or eight, and could do something around the house, then it was not usually a subsidized operation.

In a sense, it [system] survives all the way down to the 1930s in rural or small town areas. A very remarkable thing.

Q When did we get the first "welfare reform" of this system? And why?

A The first major change comes early in the 19th century. There is the growth of reasonably large cities: Philadelphia, Baltimore, New York. And this kind of neighborly surveillance and assistance by local units of government just can't suffice. When cities get to be 50,000, 80,000, people, they [governments] don't know who these people are.

So for a variety of reasons you get the institutions — the poorhouse, the workhouse, the orphanage, the insane asylums...They stick around for a long time. Three things are operating from about 1820 to 1860. One is the thought that the poor are a source of social contagion within the community and if they are isolated in institutions, then they would not infect others. The second — and this is very closely tied to early evangelical enthusiasm — was the expectation that if these folks could be put in institutions...they could be reformed. And you would know what the virtues were: thrift, hard work, prudence, temperance, all these middle-class virtues.

In the third place was the notion that public assistance saved money...I don't have to tell you things didn't work out this way. This was "welfare reform" in 1820 to 1860. These institutions survive into the 20th century. The poorhouse begins to disappear in the 1920s and '30s, but it's there for a century.

10

Photos courtesy of Social Welfare History Archives, University of Minnesota. These photos attempt to show the value of social-welfare institutions. Taken from the 1897 annual report of the Minnesota State Public School for Dependent and Neglected Children at Owatonna, they show two children as they appeared when they were received by the school; at right are the same two girls as they appeared after their stay, ready to be placed with families.

Q What were these poorhouses like?

A They were usually old houses, and there would be rooms made into dormitories. And there would be one place for the men, one place for the women and children. They were almost always at the edge of town. There was a thought that fresh air could help in the process of regeneration. And it would also remove the contagion further. It was thought they could raise vegetables, milk cows and do simple things to provide for themselves. They were heavily Protestant, of course, so there was an evening prayer very often. The meals were passable.

The thought was that they would work. But it turns out that they couldn't work because they weren't up to it. (Most were old, sick, etc.) If there was an able-bodied man, occasionally, he would be subcontracted and work on the roads or something like that. Finally, in many workhouses, they sat around picking oakum [loose fiber obtained by untwisting old ropes that, when combined with asphalt or oil, was used to caulk boat seams]...It was not a very high-class kind of labor.

Q How were conditions in the orphanages?

A The range is just enormous. It depends upon who was the manager of the orphanage, whether the organization or board of

11

directors, for example, had resources and were making a commitment and investment in those lives...These managers are frequently political appointees if they're in state orphanages. And they aren't trained, there is no training...There was no profession of child guidance or child care. It's not really until the 1880s that states beginning in Massachusetts and then Wisconsin and Minnesota and Oregon — the progressive states — begin to set up so-called Boards of Charities. They were intended to regulate and see that standards of health and education were adhered to [in the institutions].

Q When did helping poor people start to become a politically controversial issue?

A In the 19th century when you get urban and industrial forces, there is a perception that the poor are poor because their behavior is wrong. That they are lazy. That they don't save their money, that they don't plan for the future. That they drink too much. That they have too many children they can't care for. So that in the 19th century, and this is Victorian America, there is a distinction made between those who are deserving and those who are undeserving. And able-bodied men who can work are seen largely as undeserving.

The distinction is clear. The Irish and other foreigners are not worthy. They are perceived as aliens and strangers with different customs...And then, of course, in the 20th century and more recently, minorities of color play that same role.

Let me say something about African-Americans, from the Civil War to after the Emancipation Proclamation. In the South, where most of them lived until they began the migration north, they were considered to be outside of the welfare system. There were very few blacks...receiving public assistance of any sort. If these families were to survive poverty and oppression of various sorts, they had to develop their own networks. And they were networks of the extended black family and the black church.

And when Eastern European Jews came to America, they very quickly created their own [social] agencies out of the synagogue. And Italian Catholics did the same thing, and Polish Catholics; they all had their own institutions, their own old folks' homes. The Lutherans here in Minnesota established homes for worthy, aged, Lutheran men and women. So, the church played a very major role with the ethnic groups.

12

Q Do you see history repeating itself when you hear congressional leaders talk about orphanages, a bigger role for private charities, more state responsibility for the poor and other measures in their welfare reform plans?

A I don't think that there is any repetition in history. I think there is continuity...For the first 300 years of the American experience, the responsibility for public assistance was entirely an obligation of local government. The talk now about returning that financial obligation primarily to the state would be part of that continuity.

The emphasis on work is another part. It's been the American principle for centuries, the thought that persons who don't work aren't worthy. Likewise the thought that welfare reform, could, in the long run, save money. It's the same expectation welfare reformers had in the 1820s and '30s [when they created institutions]. But institutions turned out to be quite expensive.

There's an anxiety over taxpayers' dollars, whether it be in the colonial era or Victorian America or the 1990s. I have no trouble with that, but when one looks at tobacco subsidies and subsidies to the merchant marine and subsidies to homeowners of good income who can afford a large mortgage — I mean there are all kinds of handouts. But if one has property and if one is on the right side of the line, then these are not considered welfare or demeaning. That's also consistent.

Q One thing some congressional leaders have talked about is encouraging private charities to play a bigger role in helping the poor. Were there many private charities in Minnesota?

A In a city like Minneapolis there were probably 80 of them by 1900. Some were family service associations, child welfare societies, plus every [religious] denomination had its set of institutions — the old folks' homes, orphanages, their own ways of tiding over people in their congregation.

After the Great Depression, members of the Community Chest Movement — the forerunner to United Way — went to Washington and said they had no money to meet the needs. Families needed coal, or groceries, or someone to pay the rent. There was just no money left. Before that these agencies had been primarily concerned with services and not financial aid.

13

When federal money came in...it was resting on this notion of work. That was one of the strengths of the programs of the New Deal. It was better to provide work than give a handout. Handouts were demeaning...For 350 years or more, that's been the central value of the society.

Q Do you think the solutions of the past have much relevance for today?

A However strong continuity has been, the world does change. For years we've had multi-national corporations, but now they've so transformed the marketplace for labor that a lot of the old ideas don't pertain. There's a real disjunction between some of the values that we held so long, and the structure of the economy today. In 1840 to 1910, labor came to capital. All the immigrants came to America. At an accelerated pace over the [more recent] years, capital has gone to cheap labor. If you shop at Christmas time, you'll see the toys, electronics; they are made in Singapore, Taiwan, the Caribbean. These basic economic changes of production and capital control have made an enormous difference in the availability of jobs that pay enough to live above the line of poverty.

FEDERAL ASSISTANCE: IS EVERYONE ON THE DOLE?[2]

Ask Carol and Mo Aljadah whether they receive welfare, and they'll say, "Of course not!" But the middle-class couple, who live in a comfortable home in Golden Valley, Minnesota, take about $3,800 in home mortgage deductions to lower their federal tax bill each year.

Ask 69-year-old Ed Skluzacek whether his Social Security check is actually public assistance, and he'll say, "No. I worked for it." But if the retired Richfield, Minnesota, man is like many Social Security recipients, he'll get back far more from the government than he contributed.

Ask Pillsbury Inc. officials whether the company is on the dole, and they'll say no. But last year, Pillsbury received more than $1 million from a federal program to advertise and promote its corn products in Japan.

[2]Jean Hopfensperger, "Federal Assistance: Is Everyone on the Dole?," **Star Tribune**, August 27, 1995. Reprinted with permission of the **Star Tribune**, Minneapolis-St. Paul.

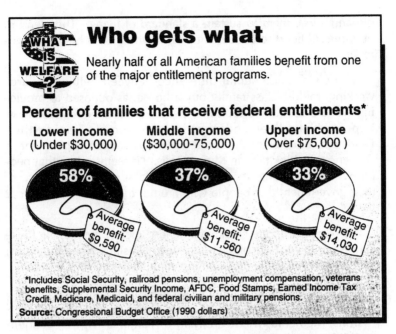

Who gets what

Nearly half of all American families benefit from one of the major entitlement programs.

Percent of families that receive federal entitlements*

Lower income
(Under $30,000)

Middle income
($30,000-75,000)

Upper income
(Over $75,000)

58%

37%

33%

Average benefit: $9,590

Average benefit: $11,560

Average benefit: $14,030

*Includes Social Security, railroad pensions, unemployment compensation, veterans benefits, Supplemental Security Income, AFDC, Food Stamps, Earned Income Tax Credit, Medicare, Medicaid, and federal civilian and military pensions.

Source: Congressional Budget Office (1990 dollars)

Star Tribune Graphic: Reprinted with permission of the *Star Tribune*, Minneapolis-St. Paul.

While most Americans consider "welfare" to be a monthly government check received by poor single parents, there is growing debate over whether the government programs that help wealthy and middle-class families and corporations are essentially the same thing.

Whether it's called welfare, an entitlement, a tax break, a subsidy or something else, most U.S. households and businesses receive some form of federal help to maintain their lifestyle or business. And in the past year, as Congress has considered more aggressive measures to balance the federal budget, some of these benefits are being scrutinized like never before.

"We tend to equate welfare with the most visible parts of it...what we don't see is how the government provides benefits to everyone in a variety of different ways," said Lawrence Jacobs, a University of Minnesota professor and social welfare specialist. "It could be a tax break to own a house, a tax break for a company's health insurance programs, retirement benefits or a public health program. These are all ways in which we try to help people and allow them to sustain a standard of living. They tend to be more subtle, discreet benefits." But others don't buy that argument.

"There's a fundamental difference between helping a hardworking, middle-class family buy a house, as opposed to providing welfare assistance for some people who are not working to improve their lives and contribute to society," said Mitch Pearlstein, director of the Center of the American Experiment, a conservative think tank in Minneapolis. "It seems to me that people who are making an effort have a claim on the assistance of their government that people who are not trying very hard do not have."

The people who are "making an effort" clearly are making those claims. A 1994 study of the main federal social welfare programs, called entitlements, by the Congressional Budget Office found:

• Nearly half of all U.S. families get government help through the major entitlement programs: Social Security and railroad pensions, Medicaid, Medicare, Aid to Families with Dependent Children (AFDC), Supplemental Security Income (SSI), veterans benefits, unemployment compensation, Earned Income Tax Credits, and federal civilian and military pensions.

• The wealthier the family, the larger the benefit. Three-fifths of families earning less than $30,000 received at least one entitlement in 1990, averaging $9,600. In contrast, one-third of families earning more than $100,000 got benefits that averaged $15,000.

Those numbers don't include the tax deductions for home mortgages, child care and health care, and they don't include the benefits that many middle-class families receive from federal student loans and other programs. "There's been a lot of discussion about welfare," Jacobs said. "There's been less discussion about the other programs that provide assistance for people who aren't poor. I suspect when the [congressional] budget cuts come home — and it becomes clear what the cuts in Medicare and Medicaid mean — people will pay more attention."

Invisible "Welfare"

Ed Skluzacek, 69, never thought his Social Security checks or Medicare had anything in common with welfare. After all, he'd contributed to the Social Security system for more than 40 years.

A welfare primer

Welfare is the word most Americans use to describe monthly checks the government gives to low-income, single parents. But the word carries a broader meaning to many social policy analysts, who use it to describe the variety of government-funded programs or tax breaks for individuals and corporations.

Q What is an "entitlement"? And why are politicians talking about them?

A Entitlements are social programs that Americans are "entitled" to if they meet the qualifications. If you're 65, for example, you're "entitled" to Social Security. The largest programs benefit the middle class — Social Security, Medicaid, Medicare, and federal military and civilian pension plans. They consume more than 75 percent of the spending. Smaller programs, designed for the poor, are Aid to Families with Dependent Children, food stamps and Supplemental Security Income.

Entitlements are in the national spotlight because they consume nearly half the federal budget — and are growing each year. Congressional budget cutters are trying to figure out how to limit them without creating political or economic upheaval.

HOME MORTGAGE DEDUCTIONS:
Welfare for the wealthy?

One of the most sacred tax breaks is the home mortgage interest deduction. But households earning $40,000 a year or less received only 6 percent of the total deductions. They make up 65 percent of the total population.

Income level	Total mortgage interest deductions
Below $10,000 (31,000 returns)	$8 million
$10-$20,000 (452,000 returns)	$186 million
$20-$30,000 (1,520,000 returns)	$781 million
$30-$40,000 (2,687,000 returns)	$1.938 billion
$40-$50,000 (3,403,000 returns)	$3.213 billion
$50-$75,000 (8,883,000 returns)	$11.245 billion
$75-$100,000 (5,130,000 returns)	$11.201 billion
$100-$200,000 (4,024,000 returns)	$14.131 billion
$200,000 and over (1,013,000 returns)	$8.457 billion
Total: 27,142,000 returns	**$51.16 billion**

Source: Joint Committee on Taxation, U.S. Congress.

ENTITLEMENT SPENDING:
A growing bite of the budget

Entitlement programs, which include Social Security, Medicaid and Medicare, consumed 47 percent of the federal budget in 1993. By the year 2003, that number is expected to reach 58 percent. Congress is attempting to limit the programs, a move likely to pinch the middle class.

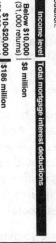

1993 mandatory federal budget spending

- Discretionary 38.6%
- Entitlements 47.3%
- Interest on debt 14.1%

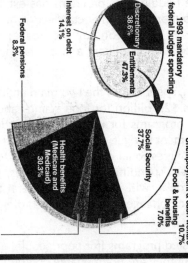

- Unemployment & cash welfare 10.7%
- Food & housing benefits 7.0%
- Social Security 37.7%
- Health benefits (Medicare and Medicaid) 30.3%
- Federal pensions 8.3%
- Other nonretirement cash 6.1%

Source: Bipartisan Commission on Entitlement and Tax Reform; Congressional Budget Office.

He estimates he put $37,000 into the system. And his employer matched those contributions. "I look at it as a wage you're paid, but never received," said Skluzacek, a former division director at the Minnesota Department of Public Service. "That $74,000 I put in could have earned a bundle [in interest] over all these years. But if I last a few more years, I'll get my money out of it."

And that's the bite, say some researchers, who note that most Americans get more money out of Social Security than they put in. Researchers say most retirees use up their contribution within four years. That's not to mention Medicare, which in Skluzacek's case has a market value of about $7,500 a year, according to estimates by the American Association of Retired Persons. Skluzacek has a daughter with a disability. She has a job, but also receives Supplemental Security Income (SSI) and Medicaid, the government health programs for the disabled and poor. What does Skluzacek see as the difference between SSI and welfare?

"Not a thing," he says. "The government gives people money and health care. And if they take a job and earn too much, they take it all away," referring to the dis-incentives of the welfare system. No one would consider the Skluzaceks, a middle-class family that enjoys golfing and volunteering at church and for charities, "welfare recipients." Yet the family benefits from four of the nation's largest social programs.

And there are so many families like the Skluzaceks that the costs of running these middle-class programs has exploded. The costs in 1993: $302 billion spent on Social Security and railroad retirement benefits; $143 billion for Medicare; $76 billion for Medicaid; $65 billion for military and civilian pensions, and $21 billion for SSI.

By comparison, spending on the two main entitlement programs for the poor was $25 billion for food stamps and $16 billion for AFDC. In fact, programs for the poor are not to blame for the exploding entitlement budget, said Sen. John Kerry, D-Mass., who last year led a congressional commission trying to figure out how to limit entitlement spending. Those programs, plus the interest on the national debt, will consume all federal tax revenues by 2012 unless policy changes are made, according to the commission's report.

"The means-tested programs [for poor people] are a problem for many reasons, but they are not the large contributor to the overall

18

growth in entitlement programs," Kerry said. "The real contributors are the middle-class entitlements, specifically Social Security, military/civil retirement and Medicaid. These are the big ones."

Mortgage Deductions

Carol and Mo Aljadah are among the 27 million taxpayers who took advantage of $51 billion in home mortgage tax deductions offered by the government last year. They consider themselves a typical middle-class family. Carol, 47, is an agent at Insurance Exchange in St. Louis Park, Minnesota; Mo, 48, is the club manager at the American Legion Post in Champlin, Minnesota. They have a 15-year-old son.

Carol said she sees home mortgage deductions not as a handout, but as an investment in the community. "The tax deductions promote home ownership, and that has a lot to do with stability and the quality of your community," she said. "And you could say that affects schools. It trickles down."

Added Mo: "I'd feel very different if I was getting a welfare check. It would be like a handout. But the mortgage is something that I paid out — it belongs to me." The Aljadahs have taken about $3,800 a year in mortgage deductions for the past five years. They deducted interest on their cabin mortgage until they paid it off. Carol says she would hate to lose the mortgage deduction.

Congress isn't talking about ending the mortgage interest deduction. But it is examining exactly who gets these deductions and how much money they make. The wealthier the household, the bigger the deduction, according to a 1994 report by the Joint Ways and Means Committee. The report found:

- Tax filers earning more than $75,000 a year take 66 percent of the total home mortgage deductions. But only 11 percent of U.S. households make that much money.

- Filers earning $40,000 a year or less received six percent of total deductions. Yet about 65 percent of U.S. households fall into that income bracket.

- Filers earning between $100,000 and $200,000 — or about two percent of households — received about 28 percent of all mortgage deductions.

Home mortgage deductions first appeared during the Civil War, when northern states levied income taxes to support the war effort, said James Gregory of the National Association of Realtors. The deductions were meant to soften the blow of the new taxes. The same was true in 1913, when the newly written U.S. tax code authorized a national income tax, he said. Mortgage deductions were included to ease the tax burden and to encourage home ownership.

Today, Congress is reconsidering at least part of that decision. The Congressional Budget Office has suggested capping mortgage deductions at $20,000, which would be the interest payment on a $250,000 to $300,000 home. That would save $23.5 billion, according to the Concord Coalition, an anti-deficit organization in Washington, D.C.

"It is increasingly hard to justify having mortgage deductions," said Martha Phillips, executive director of the Coalition. "Home ownership rates are high, but so are they in countries without them. And when you're trying to balance the budget, and you're asking all groups to give up something, how can you justify having all taxpayers kick in extra revenue so some people can live in mini-palaces? It doesn't make sense for the federal government to be subsidizing the homes of people earning $300,000 a year."

DEFINING CORPORATE WELFARE[3]

Critics have dubbed it corporate welfare, the tax breaks and subsidies received by companies that fund everything from Friskies pet food advertisements in Japan to sweet deals for mining companies using public lands. And in the past year, it has come under its most intense scrutiny. An odd political alliance ranging from presidential hopeful Sen. Phil Gramm, R-Texas, to consumer activist Ralph Nader are asking congressional budget-cutters to take the knife to programs that are being labeled anti-consumer, anti-capitalist and bad for the economy.

"We have created a social safety net for large corporations," said Stephen Moore, a research director at the Cato Institute, a libertarian think tank in Washington, D.C. "It's indefensible... There's become a consensus on the left and the right that this is an

---

[3]Jean Hopfensperger, "Scrutinizing Business Tax Breaks," **Star Tribune**, August 28, 1995. Reprinted with permission of the **Star Tribune**, Minneapolis-St. Paul.

unwise way to spend tax dollars." While business leaders hate the corporate-welfare label, they acknowledge that it's probably time for some breaks to go for the sake of reducing the federal deficit. But not all of them — not by a long shot.

"The uniform castigation of all government outlay programs is ridiculous," said Paul Huard, vice president of the National Association of Manufacturers. "It doesn't discriminate between those that have a positive effect and those that may be a total waste. We judge government programs by whether they create jobs and increase prosperity. If they don't, maybe we may stop doing them. If they do, let's keep them. It's a pretty straightforward standard." Critics say that if Congress tries to balance the budget by targeting programs for the poor, children and senior citizens, it's only fair that corporate America take some hits.

"The reason these programs are being preserved is not because they're creating jobs or making America more effective," Moore said. "It comes down to base politics and political power. Most of these grants go to Fortune 500 companies, and they have a lot of political muscle in this town. And they're flexing it."

A Hand, or a Handout?

The term "corporate welfare" has been around for years, but it wasn't openly used by government officials until recently. Labor Secretary Robert Reich threw the issue into the national spotlight when he said it was unfair to balance the budget by disproportionately cutting programs for the poor. Sixty-two percent of the midyear budget cuts — called recisions — made by Congress this summer came from programs for low-income families, according to the Center on Budget and Policy Priorities, a liberal research group.

Reich urged Washington think tanks to compile a list of "business subsidies that don't make sense." Two groups took up the challenge — the Cato Institute and the Progressive Policy Institute, a research arm of the Democratic Party. One of Nader's consumer groups, Essential Information, made its own study.

The result was the publication of a list of about 120 programs, costing taxpayers about $100 billion, that researchers labeled the "social safety net for corporations." The researchers argued that the corporate programs cost the government far more than programs for the poor; for example, the government spends about

$42 billion for food stamps and Aid to Families with Dependent Children (AFDC) combined.

Corporations insist that social welfare spending can't be compared to corporate breaks. Corporations pay taxes. They create jobs. They maintain the nation's strategic industries. Subsidies keep the United States globally competitive, supporters say, especially because many other nations heavily subsidize their industries to give them an advantage in international trade. "When the government assists development of new technology that gives people jobs, I don't regard that as welfare," Huard said. "Indeed, it's putting people to work, which is the antithesis of what people commonly view as welfare."

But some policy research groups say that's an arbitrary distinction. "A tax break is economically identical to a spending subsidy in terms of its effect," said Jeff Hammond, a policy analyst at the Progressive Policy Institute. "It's just that one appears in the budget and one does not. A tax break just is money that doesn't come in. So in many ways, a tax break is more insidious because no one knows about them unless you benefit from them."

Critics also say that corporate programs have stifled competition, provided incentives for companies to move overseas and have long outlived their usefulness. "Most of our most successful companies developed without government money," Moore said. "I reject the notion that the way to help business is to help business one by one. That's futile. We should be leveling the playing field for all business."

For example, companies that do business in Puerto Rico don't have to pay taxes on part of their earnings. The tax break was started in the early 1960s to lure business to the island, a U.S. commonwealth, but now it's used mainly by large pharmaceutical companies, Hammond said. About $3.5 billion is lost each year in taxes because of it, he said.

Other programs are simply examples of taxpayers subsidizing private industry, critics say. It's done in several ways. The government pays for research conducted by private industry to develop products that the industries eventually market. A well-publicized example is *Taxol*, a new cancer drug developed from yew trees, according to Nader researchers.

"The trees are grown on federal lands. The taxpayers pay for the research to develop and test the product; then we give the

Corporate welfare or good business?

Corporate tax breaks, subsidies and trade policies have come under growing criticism as Congress tries to find ways to balance the federal budget. Businesses say the money helps create jobs and allows them to compete with foreign companies, many of which are subsidized by their governments. Researchers critical of the programs have identified about 120 special spending and tax subsidies, which cost taxpayers about $100 billion last year. They include:

■ **$400 million** in tax deductions for **business entertainment.**

■ **$333 million** to help the nation's **auto industry** develop more fuel-efficient cars.

■ **$2 billion** in low-interest loans to **electric utility cooperatives** in rural areas, which in turn hold down the cost of running ski resorts in Aspen, Colo., and gambling casinos in Las Vegas.

■ **$500 million** to help **corporations that manufacture weapons** to export them.

■ **$500 million** in tax breaks for **companies that make ethanol,** the corn-based gasoline.

■ **$3.4 billion** in tax exemptions on income earned by **U.S. firms operating in Puerto Rico and Guam.**

■ **$140 million** to build roads in national forests so **timber companies** can remove trees.

■ **$452 million** to help **private industry,** including corporate giants such as Xerox, Dupont and Caterpillar, convert basic research into technologies with commercial potential.

■ **$390 million** to **agriculture exporters** for selling their commodities cheaply in foreign markets.

■ **$2.3 billion** in cash payments to **foreign countries** to purchase U.S. arms.

■ **$5.4 billion** in grants and loans to **foreign countries** to purchase U.S. military equipment and services, an indirect subsidy to U.S. weapon manufacturers.

■ **$1.4 billion** in tax breaks to **U.S. exporters** that are permitted to exempt part of their export income.

Sources: Cato Institute; Progressive Policy Institute; Essential Information.

Star Tribune Graphic: Reprinted with permission of the *Star Tribune*, Minneapolis-St. Paul.

rights to Bristol-Myers," said Janice Shields, a researcher for a Nader group. "And Bristol-Myers, which is expected to generate $480 million in revenues from Taxol in 1995, doesn't have to pay us any royalties for the product."

But a big chunk of the revenue that Bristol-Myers gets from Taxol will go to the government in corporate income taxes, argue program supporters. Likewise, the government pays for the construction of many of the roads used by the timber industry to harvest trees in national forests. In the past 20 years, the Forest Service has built 340,000 miles of roads, more than eight times the length of the interstate highway system, primarily for logging companies, according to the Cato Institute.

Some of the biggest breaks go to international business, military contractors, high-technology industries and agribusiness. Last year, these breaks included:

- $5.4 billion in loans and grants to foreign countries to buy U.S. military equipment services and weapons — what critics say is an indirect subsidy to arms manufacturers.

- $400 million in tax deductions for business entertainment expenses.

- $452 million to help private industry, including corporate giants such as Xerox Corp., DuPont and Caterpillar Inc., convert research technology into commercial products.

That's not to mention the deals that the U.S. government gives to concessionaires at national parks, cattle ranchers who use public lands and mining companies that pay no royalties to the federal treasury on millions of dollars of earnings, the reports say.

Companies Defend Breaks

Minnesota corporations that receive government funding are annoyed by the corporate-welfare label, but many agree that some of the issues raised by critics are worth discussion. "Words like 'corporate welfare' make it difficult to have the kind of reasoned debate and discussion of these important issues," said Garland West, spokesman for Cargill Inc. of Minnetonka. "Unfortunately, we've gotten into a political discussion where buzzwords substitute for reasoned discussion. We need to get away from it."

Mike Shannon, vice chairman of Ecolab Inc., of St. Paul and a board member of the National Association of Manufacturers, agrees that the term polarizes the issue. But, he adds, "There's a certain fit. Basically, what are being categorized as items of corporate welfare relate to policies issued by the federal government at various points in history to [give incentive to] corporations to do a variety of things," Shannon said. "In some cases, the time has probably passed where those incentives made sense. In some cases, those incentives don't work. In some cases, those incentives may be overly generous. So in that context, I think it's appropriate for them to [be] reviewed."

One of the programs that officials at Cargill want to see reviewed is the Export Enhancement Program (EEP). Under the program, Cargill has received $1.29 billion in cash bonuses from the government over the past decade to export its grain to certain countries at below-cost prices. Cargill is the top beneficiary of the program, according to reports. But even Cargill officials don't support keeping the program.

"The EEP has been something we've consistently opposed since the 1980s because it runs counter to the interest of American agriculture," West said. "It doesn't develop long-term demand for products. It's depressing the price. It's become a market management tool. In effect, it puts the government in the position of being able to decide what commodity will be sold, to whom and at what price."

Meanwhile, companies such as Pillsbury of Minneapolis get money from a much-maligned government program that pays corporations for their advertisements and market promotions overseas. In 1992, for example, U.S. taxpayers paid $10 million promoting Sunkist oranges, $1.2 million boosting the sales of American Legend mink coats and $465,000 advertising McDonald's Chicken McNuggets, according to the Cato Institute.

Pillsbury spokesman Terry Thompson said the Market Promotion Program has done precisely what it was created to do for Pillsbury — it opened a new market, namely corn in Japan. And that benefits everyone, from the farmers who plant the corn to Pillsbury employees, he said. "The program has enabled us to introduce a product and develop a business in Japan," Thompson said. "It has improved jobs, and it's good for agriculture in one state. From 1986 to 1991, the total acreage of sweet corn planted by independent Idaho growers...increased from 9,500 to 13,600.

That's directly related to this program. On the other hand, if the program was suspended, we can live with it."

Honeywell Inc. of Minneapolis is another Minnesota firm that receives money from a half-dozen government agencies — for research. The money is used to develop everything from advanced cockpits for commercial airliners to communication systems for the Defense Department, said Ron Peterson, vice president of technology for Honeywell.

Last year, Honeywell received an $8 million grant to design production controls for oil refineries and industrial plants, said Peterson. It was paid for by the government's Advance Technology Program, which underwrites new technology with commercial potential. Critics say companies should pay for the research themselves because they ultimately profit from any new technology discovered. The Honeywell research, for example, is designed to address unforeseen shutdowns that cost private oil companies $20 billion a year, Peterson said.

Peterson said it makes sense for the government to pay for the research, which is usually too high-risk for a company to underwrite on its own. "The value of a lot of research is much, much broader than any one company can get benefits from," Peterson said, "If you invent...a transistor, for example, the value to society as a whole and to companies in the same field are often 100 or 1,000 times bigger than the benefits any one company would get from it. And clearly, it makes us more competitive as a nation."

The Battle Continues

Throughout the summer, Congress has debated funding for some of the most controversial corporate programs. Although there was some tinkering, none was eliminated. Critics were disappointed, but say they are optimistic that corporate programs are heading for the chopping block as the pressure increases to balance the federal budget.

"They're such a huge and pervading part of our budget, they become the last great component of federal spending to get to before we get to entitlements," Moore said. "It should be easier to cut the social safety net for McDonald's than to cut programs for seniors and other groups that receive entitlements. I think that will become clear to Congress."

Business leaders agree that many of the special programs will end. "We're prepared to live with some cuts," said Huard, of the National Association of Manufacturers. "But they'll have to pick and choose in a discriminating fashion." Whatever Congress does, it will be monitored closely by a small but determined group. The Cato Institute and the Progressive Policy Institute say they'll be producing an end-of-the-year score card on Congress' progress on the issue. And a group of liberal members of Congress last month began the Gilded Lily Award for Corporate Welfare. They plan to make monthly awards for what they consider the most egregious examples of federal subsidies for private business.

"It's an issue that's not going to go away," Moore said.

CHAPTER 1

THE WELFARE POLICY DEBATE

THE WELFARE SYSTEM HAS FAILED

Robert Rector

Robert Rector is a Senior Policy Analyst at the Heritage Foundation, Washington, D.C. The Heritage Foundation is a public policy institute, which publishes articles and lobbies Congress to promote conservative economic and social policies.

■ POINTS TO CONSIDER

1. How did Johnson's "War on Poverty" of the 1960s affect welfare spending?

2. Summarize the correlations Rector makes between welfare spending and societal trends, such as out-of-wedlock births. Does he show a causal relationship?

3. What does the author believe the goals of future welfare programs should be?

4. Discuss the proposals made for welfare reform. Contrast those with current policies.

Excerpted from the testimony of Robert Rector before the Senate Finance Committee, March 9, 1995.

Since the onset of the War on Poverty, the U.S. has spent over $5.3 trillion on welfare.

The War on Poverty has failed. It has been thirty years since President Lyndon Johnson launched his "unconditional war." But in most respects, the problems of the poor, the underclass and the inner city have actually gotten worse, not better, in the subsequent years.

This failure is not due to a lack of spending. In 1993, federal, state and local governments spent $324 billion on means-tested welfare programs for low income Americans. Welfare now absorbs 5% of GDP, up from 1.5% in 1965 when the War on Poverty began. Though Johnson declared that "the days of the dole are numbered," welfare now involves an ever-expanding share of the population. Today nearly one out of seven American children is enrolled in AFDC with Uncle Sam's welfare check serving as a surrogate father. About half of the children currently on AFDC will remain on welfare for over ten years.

Swollen AFDC rolls are in turn a response to rising illegitimacy; two out of three black children in the U.S. are now born out of wedlock, up from around 25% when the War on Poverty began. Rapid increases in illegitimacy are also occurring among low income whites; the illegitimate birth rate among white high school drop-outs is 48%. Overall, over 30% of American children are now born to single mothers.

The core feature of the U.S. welfare system, and its central problem, is that it subsidizes and thus promotes self-destructive behavior. Specifically, the welfare system promotes: non-work, illegitimacy, and divorce. Welfare, insidiously, creates its own clientele; by undermining work ethic and family structure, the welfare state generates a growing population in "need of aid." Welfare bribes individuals into courses of behavior which in the long run are self-defeating to the individual, harmful to children, and increasingly, a threat to society.

A dramatic reform, reversing the trends of the last thirty years, is required. Real reform would convert welfare from a one way hand-out into a system of mutual responsibility in which welfare recipients would be given aid but would be expected to contribute something back to society for assistance given. A reformed system must strongly discourage dependency and irresponsible behavior and encourage constructive behavior. It must firmly control soaring welfare costs which are slowly bankrupting the nation. Finally, and most importantly, welfare reform must reduce the illegitimate birth rate in the U.S. and promote the formation of stable two-parent families. Any "reform" which does not dramatically reduce the illegitimate birth rate will not save money and will fail to truly help America's children and society.

TOTAL WELFARE SPENDING

Total federal and state spending on welfare programs was $324.3 billion in FY 1993. Of the total, $234.3 billion or 72% comes from federal funding and $90 billion or 28% comes from state or local funds. But these figures significantly understate the role of the federal government in welfare. Many federal welfare programs require a state government contribution; in order for individuals within a state to receive aid from these federal programs, the state government must match or pay a certain share of federal spending in the state on that program. Out of the total of $90 billion in state and local welfare spending described in this paper, fully $78.6 billion takes the form of state and local contributions to federally created welfare programs. Of total welfare spending of $324 billion, only $11.4 billion or 3.5% is spending for independent state welfare programs.

CATEGORIES OF WELFARE SPENDING

As noted, the welfare system theoretically is designed to promote three proclaimed goals: to prop up material living standards; to promote self-sufficiency; and to expand economic opportunities within low-income communities. Federal and state governments operate a variety of welfare programs to meet these goals. Such programs include: cash aid programs; food programs; medical aid programs; housing aid programs; energy aid programs; jobs and training programs; targeted and means-tested education programs; social service programs; and urban and community development programs.

Cash Aid: The federal government operates eight major means-tested cash assistance programs. Many state governments also operate independent cash programs termed General Assistance or General Relief. Total cash welfare spending by federal and state governments reached $71.5 billion in FY 1993.

Food Aid: The federal government operates 11 major programs providing food assistance to low income persons. Total food aid

31

to low income persons equalled $36 billion in FY 1993.

Housing Aid: The federal government runs 14 major housing programs for low income persons. Many state governments also operate independent state public housing programs. Total housing aid for low income persons equalled $23.5 billion in FY 1993.

Medical Aid: The federal government runs eight medical programs for low income persons. Many states operate independent medical General Assistance programs. Total medical aid equalled $155.8 billion in FY 1993.

Energy Aid: The federal government operates two programs to help pay the energy bills or to insulate the homes of persons with low incomes. Total spending equalled $1.6 billion in FY 1993.

Education Aid: The federal government runs 10 programs providing educational assistance to low income persons, disadvantaged minorities, or low-income communities. Total spending equalled $17.3 billion in FY 1993.

Training and Jobs Programs: The federal government currently operates nine different jobs and training programs for low income persons, costing $5.3 billion in FY 1993.

Targeted and Means-Tested Social Services: The federal government also runs 11 programs providing special social services to low income persons. These programs cost $8.4 billion in FY 1993.

Urban and Community Aid Programs: The federal government runs five programs to aid economically distressed communities. These programs cost $4.8 billion in FY 1993.

THE GROWTH OF THE WELFARE STATE

The welfare state, after remaining at low levels through the 1950's and early 1960's, has undergone explosive growth since the onset of the War on Poverty. In inflation adjusted terms, welfare spending has grown in every year except one since the mid-sixties.

• In constant dollars federal, state and local governments now spend nine times as much on welfare as in 1964 when the War on Poverty was beginning. Welfare spending per capita in constant dollars is seven times as high as in 1964.

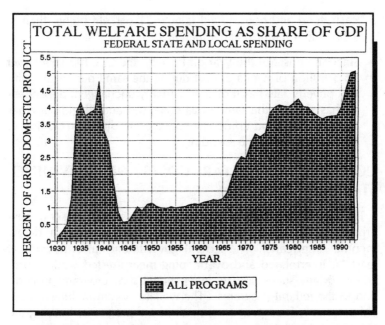

Source: Heritage Foundation in Congressional testimony by Robert Rector, March 9, 1995.

- After adjusting for inflation, welfare spending per capita today is five times as high as during the Great Depression when a quarter of the work force was unemployed.

- Welfare spending is absorbing an ever greater share of the national economy. In 1964 welfare spending equaled 1.23 percent of Gross Domestic Product. By 1993, spending had risen to 5.1 percent of GDP; This was a record high, exceeding the previous peak set during the Great Depression.

- Welfare spending in FY 1991, FY 1992, FY 1993 exceeded defense spending for the first time since the 1930's.

- There are repeated claims that Ronald Reagan "slashed" welfare spending. In reality welfare spending grew during the 1980's, after adjusting for inflation. In 1993, per capita welfare spending in constant dollars was 43 percent higher than when President Reagan took office in 1980.

- Contrary to some claims, the growth in welfare spending has not been limited to medical aid. In constant dollars, per capita cash, food and housing aid is now 31 percent higher than in 1980 and 4.6 times higher than in 1964.

- Since the onset of the War on Poverty, the U.S. has spent over $5.3 trillion on welfare. But during the same period, the official poverty rate has remained virtually unchanged; dependency has soared; the family has collapsed and illegitimacy has skyrocketed. And crime has escalated in direct proportion to the growth in welfare spending.

CONTROLLING WELFARE COSTS AND PROVIDING STATE FLEXIBILITY

The U.S. welfare system may be defined as the total set of government programs explicitly designed to assist poor and low income Americans. The federal government currently runs at least 76 interrelated and overlapping means-tested welfare programs. Many states operate independent state programs in addition to the federal programs. The welfare system includes: cash aid programs; food programs; medical aid programs; housing aid programs; energy aid programs; jobs and training programs; targeted and means-tested education programs; social service programs; and urban and community development programs.

From the start of the War on Poverty in 1965 to the present, welfare spending has cost the taxpayers $5.3 trillion in constant 1993 dollars. This is greater than the cost of defeating Germany and Japan in World War II, after adjusting for inflation.

Moreover, there is not even the faintest glimmer of "light at the end of the tunnel" for the end of the War on Poverty. According to the Congressional Budget Office, total annual means-tested welfare spending will rise to $538 billion and six percent of GDP by 1999. By that year the U.S. will be spending more than two dollars on welfare for each dollar spent on national defense. While a major portion of the projected growth of welfare spending is for medical services, other programs will show steady growth as well. For example, spending on cash, food, and housing programs are projected to grow by over a third during the next five years.

Solution: *End Welfare Entitlements, Convert Separate Means-tested Programs into a Welfare Block Grant, and Cap the Growth of Welfare Spending at the Rate of Inflation.* The long history of bogus welfare reforms, all of which were promised to save money

34

but did not, leads one to the obvious conclusion. The only way to limit the growth of welfare spending is to do just that: limit the growth of welfare spending. The welfare system must be put on a diet.

Welfare entitlements should be ended. Most separate federal non-medical welfare programs should be eliminated and the funds should be pooled into a single welfare block grant to the states. The future growth of federal non-medical means-tested welfare spending should then be capped at three percent per annum. Comprehensive reform along these lines is provided in: "The Welfare Reform Act of 1994" (S.2134) introduced by Senators Lauch Faircloth, Charles Grassley and Hank Brown and the companion bill H.R. 4566 introduced by Jim Talent, Tim Hutchinson and Charles Canady in the House of Representatives.

Similarly the entitlement nature of Medicaid should be eliminated. Medicaid and other means-tested medical programs should be converted into a single medical block grant to the states which would increase at the rate of medical inflation. Block granting medical and non-medical means-tested programs and restricting the growth in funding to the respective rates of inflation would save roughly $150 billion over the next five years.

By slowing the outpouring from the federal welfare spigot, such a welfare spending limit would gradually reduce the subsidization of dysfunctional behavior: dependency, non-work, and illegitimacy. The spending controls would send a warning signal to state welfare bureaucracies. Cushioned by a steady and increasing flow of federal funds in the past, most bureaucracies have found no need to grapple with the tough and controversial policies needed to really reduce illegitimacy and dependency. With a cap on the growth of future federal funds, state governments would, for the first time, be forced to adopt innovative and aggressive policies that would reduce the welfare rolls.

While such a block grant approach would give the state governments infinitely more flexibility than the current system, we should not have a system of "zero responsibility block grants." The use of federal block grant funds must be governed by a few basic moral and structural principles established at the federal level.

THE WELFARE SYSTEM HAS NOT FAILED

Robert Greenstein

Robert Greenstein is Executive Director of the Center on Budget and Public Priorities. The Center, located in Washington, D.C., lobbies Congress to promote progressive economic and social policies.

■ POINTS TO CONSIDER

1. Give examples of highly successful means-tested programs.

2. Assess the changes in family structure over the past thirty years and their effects on the welfare system, according to Greenstein.

3. Why does the author distinguish between cash assistance and other non-cash benefits such as Medicaid when discussing poverty levels?

4. Discuss the effects of economic changes on poverty levels. Compare the effectiveness of anti-poverty programs in the period of 1964-73 with that of the 1980s.

Excerpted from the testimony of Robert Greenstein before the Senate Finance Committee, March 9, 1995.

Between 1964 and 1973, when a strong economy was coupled with more generous antipoverty programs, the poverty rate fell from 19 percent to 11 percent.

Robert Rector of the Heritage Foundation has stated in congressional testimony that "Since the onset of the War on Poverty, the U.S. has spent over $5.3 trillion on welfare. But during the same period, the official poverty rate has remained virtually unchanged." In order to arrive at the $5.3 trillion figure, "welfare spending" must be broadly defined to include spending on all means-tested programs, even those programs that confer a significant amount of benefits on families above the poverty line.

Rector's suggestion that "welfare spending" has accomplished little, as evidenced by his claim that the poverty rate has remained virtually unchanged, misses several key points. First, between 1964 and 1973, when a strong economy was coupled with more generous antipoverty programs, the poverty rate fell from 19 percent to 11 percent. Second, the upward drift in the poverty rate over the past 15 years appears primarily to reflect changes in the economy — most notably, declining wages. Third, the official poverty rate data only measures cash income. It does not include benefits from poverty programs that provide benefits in-kind such as Medicaid, and food and housing programs. Yet the bulk of the increase in antipoverty spending in recent decades has been in the in-kind programs. These programs cannot be said to have failed in reducing poverty when they are not counted in measuring poverty.

To come to a figure of $5.3 trillion, "welfare spending" has to be broadly defined to include any means-tested program, including programs in which a significant amount of the benefits go to families above the poverty line. As noted earlier, such a definition goes far beyond the common conception of "welfare." Furthermore, when considering what such a figure means, it is important to place it in context.

- Between 1964 and 1994, the federal government spent a total of more than $31 trillion (in 1993 inflation-adjusted dollars). Total GDP over that period equaled almost $143 trillion.

- Even if one accepts Rector's definition of "welfare spending," his figure suggests that 16 percent of total federal spending — and 4 percent of total GDP — over the past 30 years was spent on means-tested programs.

- Combined federal spending since 1964 on AFDC, Medicaid, SSI, and the major nutrition entitlement programs totaled about $2 trillion. While this is a large dollar amount, it amounts to less than 1.5 percent of total GDP and about 6.6 percent of total federal outlays over that period.

- Spending on AFDC alone over this 30 year period totaled less than 1.5 percent of federal outlays.

SPENDING AND POVERTY

Rector also suggests that this spending has been of little worth because he claims the official poverty rate has remained virtually unchanged since the War on Poverty began. This statement is problematic for several reasons.

First, a large fraction of this spending consists of programs that assist families without increasing their cash incomes. Since non-cash benefits are not counted in the official measurement of poverty, the effects of these programs do not show up in the poverty statistics. This, therefore, provides no evidence that such programs are ineffective. For example, programs like food stamps help families purchase food but do not reduce officially measured poverty. Similarly, Medicaid does not increase a recipient's cash income, but it does provide an important service and should not be considered a "failure" because it does not affect the official poverty statistics.

Moreover, many programs that assist low-income people were not designed to foster self-sufficiency or help families work their way out of poverty. For example, Medicaid does not provide skills training for recipients; rather, it provides health care coverage for many people who could not otherwise afford it. Medicaid should not be expected to reduce poverty rates directly.

The WIC program provides another example of a highly successful means-tested program that does not directly reduce the official poverty rate. The WIC program provides coupons for specific foods to low-income pregnant and postpartum women, infants and children under age five. To be eligible for WIC, low-income women, infants and children must be found to be at nutritional risk for medical or dietary reasons. WIC is widely regarded as one of the most successful of all federal programs. A multi-year, national evaluation conducted by the U.S. Department of Agriculture during the Reagan Administration found that WIC markedly reduces infant deaths, low birthweight, and premature births. WIC also is associated with higher immunization rates and increased use of prenatal and pediatric care.

Also of note, some programs that do provide cash assistance provide benefit levels so low that they reduce the severity of poverty but do not lift households out of poverty. The average AFDC family of three receives maximum benefits equal to 42 percent of the poverty line. Even if one uses an unofficial measure of poverty that considers the value of non-cash assistance such as food stamps, free school lunches, and housing aid in addition to cash assistance such as AFDC or SSI, these combined benefits often are not enough to lift the poor above the poverty line. For example, only about 18 percent of the poor were lifted above the poverty line by cash assistance, food stamps, and housing aid in 1992. These programs, however, reduced the depth of poverty for many more poor people. In fact, these benefits reduced the "poverty gap" — the total amount by which the incomes of poor families fall below the poverty line — by some 42 percent in 1992.

Since 1977, however, the poverty rate has drifted upward. In 1977, some 11.6 percent of the population was poor. In 1993, the poverty rate stood at 15.1 percent. The years 1977 and 1993 are appropriate years to compare because they came at similar points in the economic cycle. The major factor behind the upward drift in poverty appears to be fundamental shifts in the economy and not excessively generous anti-poverty programs. Since the late 1970s, falling wages and declining job opportunities for lower-skilled workers contributed to rising poverty rates.

• In 1979, some 12.1 percent of full-time year-round workers earned too little to lift a family of four out of poverty (1977 data are not available). By 1993, some 16.2 percent of these workers had earnings this low. The average hourly wages for non-supervisory jobs also fell by 14 percent from 1977 to 1993, after adjusting for inflation.

• Similarly, in 1993, the proportion of families with children in which the head of the household worked but the family was still poor stood at 11.4 percent; by contrast, in 1977, some 7.7 percent of such families were poor.

In addition to declining labor market prospects for those at the bottom of the income spectrum, changes in family structure have contributed to the increase in poverty. Female-headed families were both a larger proportion of all families and of poor families in 1993 than in the late 1970s. At the same time, however, the effect of the growing number of female-headed families on pover-ty trends in the past 20 years is sometimes exaggerated. During this period, the average size of female-headed families became smaller and poverty also increased among two-parent families. As a result of these and other trends, the proportion of poor people living in female-headed families has remained fairly steady since the late 1970s. Census data show that 37.2 percent of all poor people lived in female-headed families in 1977. In 1993, this fig-ure had increased only modestly to 39.4 percent.

A weaker safety net also has contributed to the rise in poverty for some groups. In 1993, fewer than one in every seven children who were poor before receipt of government benefits was lifted from poverty by cash benefits. In 1979, nearly one in five chil-dren who was poor before receipt of cash benefits was lifted from poverty by them. (These data are not available for 1977.)

WHAT IS THE VALUE OF BENEFITS PROVIDED TO AFDC FAMILIES?

There is often confusion surrounding the issue of the value of benefits families on AFDC receive, with some claiming that these families typically receive benefits totaling $15,000. The income most recipients have to meet their basic needs is, in fact, modest, leaving families well below the poverty line.

- In 1994, the average AFDC family of three was eligible for a maximum of $415 per month, or $4,980 per year, in cash assistance. Nearly three-quarters of all AFDC families included three or fewer members.

- Most AFDC families also receive food stamps. A family of three that received $415 in AFDC benefits would receive about $249 in food stamps.

- Together, an average AFDC family of three receives a maximum of $664 per month, or $7,968 per year, in food stamp and AFDC benefits. This represents two-thirds of the poverty line.

- Average AFDC and food stamp benefits combined have fallen by more than one-quarter over the past two decades and have now receded to the level of AFDC benefits alone in 1960, before the food stamp program was created.

AFDC recipients, however, do receive other benefits and services in addition to food stamps. Most notably, AFDC recipients are "categorically eligible" for Medicaid.

Medicaid provides an important service to AFDC families. However, it is inappropriate to count Medicaid costs as "income" for families on AFDC. Medicaid payments go to doctors and hospitals, not AFDC recipients, and cannot be used to meet basic expenses such as food, shelter and clothing. Furthermore, a family that has numerous medical problems and, consequently, produces higher Medicaid costs for the government does not have more "income" with which to pay rent than a similar family receiving AFDC that does not have such high medical expenses. Including Medicaid in the calculations of the income available to AFDC recipients would be inconsistent with how other health assistance is described; most employed individuals do not consider the value of their employer-provided health care coverage when stating their income level. And few favor including the value of such coverage in their taxable income.

In addition to Medicaid, some AFDC families receive nutrition assistance through the WIC program, the School Lunch Program, the Low-Income Home Energy Assistance Program (LIHEAP), and subsidized housing. Unlike Medicaid (which provides medical insurance), these programs are more like cash assistance — they help families meet monthly budgets. But benefits in WIC, the school lunch program, and LIHEAP are modest. And while housing benefits are larger, most AFDC families do not receive them. Only one-quarter of AFDC recipients receive housing assistance. AFDC recipients may participate in other programs, such as education or training programs, but these do not typically provide cash or cash-like assistance.

The three-quarters of families receiving AFDC who do not receive housing assistance must pay for food, clothing, shelter, and transportation with a family income that averages between $8,000 and $9,000 per year for a family of three, depending on whether the family receives WIC, free school meals, and LIHEAP. When one factors in the average amount that AFDC families receiving housing assistance appear to save on housing costs, even these families remain below the poverty line.

CONCLUSION

While many point to government spending on low-income programs as the cause of rising entitlement costs and budget deficits, non-medical means-tested programs are not exploding in cost nor do they provide excessive benefits to poor families. Nearly all agree that the welfare system needs fundamental reform, but misperceptions about "welfare" spending should not drive the policy debate.

READING

4

PROMOTING SELF-SUFFICIENCY

Glenn C. Loury

Glenn C. Loury is a Professor of Economics at Boston University. He specializes in the study of national problems of social disorder. His particular concern is the issue of out-of-wedlock births.

■ POINTS TO CONSIDER

1. Discuss the findings of the 1965 Moynihan Report and its significance to the welfare reform debate today.

2. According to the author, what roles do marriage and family play in establishing "social capital"? Discuss the gender implications of this.

3. How has the public policy view of welfare shifted? What do critics and the general public have to say about this shift?

4. Restate the "root" of the problems in low-income areas as cited in the reading. Are there gender and race issues involved in this? Explain.

Excerpted from the prepared statement of Glenn C. Loury, presented to the Subcommittee on Human Resources of the House Ways and Means Committee, January 20, 1995.

It is now widely accepted that placing upon welfare recipients the obligation to engage in activities which limit their dependence is necessary and legitimate public policy.

Of course, most Americans know this instinctively, without having to be told by social scientists. Indeed, concern about problems of family disruption has been an important social issue at least since 1965, when now Senator Moynihan issued his famous report on the "Negro Family." By daring to suggest that dysfunctional family behavior among poor blacks constituted an unsuperable barrier to economic equality, Moynihan elicited an emotional, ideologically-charged response which permanently altered racial discourse in America. The now-familiar indictment, "blaming the victim" literally was invented in reaction to Moynihan's argument. A dear price was paid for this response, though not by those who led the charge.

What in the 1960s was a question about black society has in the 1990s become critical for all Americans. Charles Murray has announced to much fanfare the coming of the white underclass. Having essentially written-off the black community as a lost cause — with an illegitimacy rate nationwide near two-thirds, and even higher in the inner-city, politicians and scholars come now to contemplate what might be done to save the rest of America. The answer seems to be that we must place greater emphasis on "values." And, while I am all in favor of this, I am less than sanguine that the fix will be so easy.

People are not automata; their behavior in matters sexual may not be easily manipulated by changing their marginal tax rates or their recipiency status under welfare programs. It is my conviction that the problems of illegitimacy and family breakdown are, at base, cultural and moral problems, which require broad societal action in addition to legislative change. The emergence of morally authoritative public leadership can have only a small effect here, and is unlikely to occur in any event. Yet, in every community there are agencies of moral and cultural development which seek to shape the ways in which individuals conceive of their duties to themselves, of their obligations to each other, and of their responsibilities before God. These mainly though not exclusively religious institutions are the natural sources of legitimate moral teaching — indeed, the only sources. If these institutions are not restored, through the devoted agency of the people

45

and not their government, then the behavioral problems which Moynihan first noticed thirty years ago will persist, threatening the survival of our republic.

MARRIAGE AS SOCIAL CAPITAL

In my early writing on economic inequality in American society I introduced the concept of "social capital." Many others have found this a useful notion, and it is now in wide use in the social sciences. The term emphasizes the importance for economic development of non-economic resources. It refers to aspects of social organization (families, social networks, adolescent peer groups) that help individuals to act for their own economic benefit. The term also captures the idea that the institutional infrastructure within a given community (civic and religious organizations) helps to empower individuals for participation in economic and political life, and that the ideals and values which are transmitted and reinforced through social mechanisms can impact powerfully on economic performance. The point is that the extent and quality of relationships among persons can usefully be conceived as an economic asset, in some cases as important as physical or financial capital for determining whether or not a community can prosper.

The process by which a person moves from childhood to becoming an effective adult is like a production process. The output, a citizen, is produced from inputs of education, parental attention and concern, acculturation, nutrition, etc. Some of these inputs are bought and sold on markets, but many of the relevant inputs become available to the developing person only as the byproduct of non-economic activities. Parental attention and concern, for example, accrue to a youngster as the consequence of the social relations which operate between mother and father, and their respective families. So, within any community a crucial resource needed to produce tomorrow's citizens is the quality of social ties between today's men and women of child-bearing age. This is an elemental social fact.

In a recent essay in *Policy Review*, anthropologist David Murray has documented the extent to which all human societies develop norms surrounding the bearing and raising of children which respect this elemental social fact. He stresses the universal recognition of marriage, and child bearing within marriage, as a means of domesticating — one could also say of civilizing — young males. "Neighborhoods without fathers are seedbeds for preda-

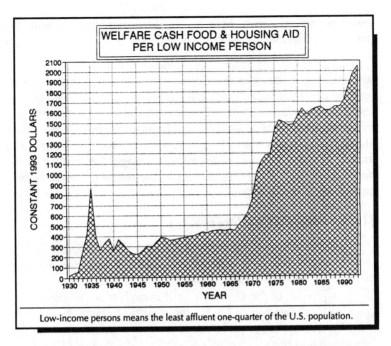

Source: Heritage Foundation in Congressional testimony by Robert Rector, March 9, 1995.

tors," writes Murray. George Gilder has also stressed this theme. Communities in which the vast majority of families consist of women without men who consider themselves responsible for their children, tend to be "under-capitalized" in a resource vital for social development.

This is, in my judgment, a central reason for the economic and social problems besetting inner-city communities today. As Gilder has recently written, "Society is continually beset by an invasion of 'barbarians,' i.e., teenaged boys. Unless they are tamed by marriage and the provider role, they become enemies of civilization. Males rule, whether through economic power as in civilized societies, or through violent coercion by the male gangs in the inner city (a so-called matriarchy where mothers cower in locked apartments, terrorized by their sons.) Thus, it is crucial to consider the impact of the welfare state on the socialization of young men." I am saying here that marriage should be seen as an important form of social capital. In the absence of marriage, and the joining of families which marriage represents, there are simply fewer people around to help a struggling young couple with the overwhelming task of raising children.

Moreover, the "legitimacy" of children is an important concept. Anthropologist Murray refers to it as "nothing less than the orderly transfer of social meaning across the generations." The Harvard sociologist Orlando Patterson has elaborated a persuasive and influential theory of slavery, in which the concept of "natal alienation" — the separation of close relations between children and their forebears — plays a key role. Marriage, by creating legitimate children, ties families of people together into mutually supportive social relationships.

THE INNER-CITY CONTEXT

I would like to explore more fully the inner-city social context within which the problems of out-of-wedlock births manifest themselves. Perhaps our best guide in this matter is ethnographer Elijah Anderson of the University of Pennsylvania. Anderson has been a close observer of life on the streets of ghetto America for nearly a quarter-century. His recent work is based on extended interviews and observation in a North Philadelphia neighborhood. He relies heavily on the concept of "the streets," the physical and social milieu in which people interact. In these poor communities the physical environment is dilapidated, dirty, unsafe, unkempt, noisy. Young people spend a lot of time "in the streets," day and night. The streets are full of women and children. Men, especially, in the roles of husbands, are scarce. Quoting Anderson: "The demoralization and deterioration of the neighborhood are omnipresent: open-air drug sales, numerous pregnant girls, incivility, crime, many street kids, few up-standing residents."

VALUES, PUBLIC POLICY, AND THE STATE

It is now widely accepted that placing upon welfare recipients the obligation to engage in activities which limit their dependence is necessary and legitimate public policy. Far from being punitive, as some liberal critics of this proposal allege, the imposition of such obligation represents a keeping of faith with a social accord of mutual expectation. The key point to recognize is that the state cannot escape the necessity to communicate some moral message by the actions it takes, even if only by default. The failure to impose obligations on recipients is also an action, which signals what is valued in society.

The audience for these normative messages is not limited to the set of people directly affected, but extends to the entire population. Indeed, sustaining political support for public provision to the needy requires the maintenance of some compatibility between the values expressed through the policy, and the beliefs broadly held by the public. The conduct of public policy also communicates something to the citizenry at large about the moral standing of those persons directly reached by policy. In the case of welfare, structuring assistance so that it leads to the eventual attainment of self-sufficiency by recipients actually shows respect for the subjects of state action, and enhances the dignity of these persons.

CONCLUSION

I believe these considerations are especially critical for black Americans to recognize. For, when one considers the great problems of our inner-cities, it is inescapable that at the root of these problems lie dysfunctional behaviors of citizens which ultimately are not amenable to state-sponsored remedy. This means, in my opinion, that the intellectual, religious and civic leadership of these communities must embrace their responsibilities to provide moral leadership, to an even greater extent than is already being done. Black leaders must work, with public officials and with other Americans of good will, to build communal institutions that can instill in our youngsters a normative framework sufficient to allow them to partake of the great opportunities which this society offers.

READING

5

PUNISHING THE POOR

Rosemary Radford Ruether

Rosemary Radford Ruether teaches theology at Garrett-Evangelical Theological Seminary in Evanston, Illinois.

■ POINTS TO CONSIDER

1. Discuss the inadequacy of social welfare programs.

2. What is the image of the poor and how has this image driven the public policy debate on welfare?

3. Summarize the statistical information on welfare recipients.

4. Describe the author's proposals for welfare reform. Contrast those with other proposals for welfare reform.

Mary Radford Ruether, "Welfare 'Reforms' Aim at Punishing Poor," **National Catholic Reporter**, 3 June 1994: 17. Reprinted with permission, **National Catholic Reporter**, Kansas City MO. Subscriptions: 1-800-333-7373.

Eighty percent of welfare recipients receive benefits for only two years and 50 percent are off welfare within one year.

Amid the shadow of the debate on health care reform has begun a second, less-noticed debate on welfare reform that deserves more attention from those concerned with justice in America.

The United States has been tardy in developing government assistance to the poor, and its programs have remained minimal compared with European industrialized countries. It has continued to maintain a suspicious and punitive attitude toward poor people, viewing their poverty as personal failure rather than a problem of the economic system.

Public assistance to the poor has been seen as public charity, rather than a basic right of all citizens to a minimum standard of life's necessities. Welfare caseworkers are poorly paid, given an excessive caseload and an inordinate amount of paperwork and required to investigate the assets and social relations of the applicants in a way that puts them in an adversarial relation to those they are supposed to "help."

Public assistance had developed and been expanded in the United States in times of social crisis but has been kept at a level well below the federal poverty line, which is itself unrealistically low. Aid to Dependent Children was one of the programs initiated under the Social Security Act of 1935 along with the Social Security system of retirement pensions, aid to the aged, blind and disabled and unemployment compensation. It was expanded to become Aid to Families with Dependent Children in 1950, giving a family grant primarily to unemployed women with dependent children without a male breadwinner.

The outcry against poverty and hunger in the United States in the 1960s brought new programs of food aid, food stamps and supplemental nutritional programs for recent mothers and undernourished children as well as Medicare and Medicaid, various job-training programs and early education experiments, such as Head Start.

In the 1980s, under the Reagan and Bush administrations, federal assistance for all those programs was drastically cut and the states were forced to assume a larger percentage of the costs. Millions of people were dropped from the welfare rolls or had their checks for food stamps reduced. Mother and child nutrition programs, funds for school lunches, job training for youths and Head Start all were slashed by Presidents who at the same time escalated the military budgets to more than $300 billion annually and reduced taxes for the wealthy. The impression was given that public assistance was far too costly and "didn't work," creating a population of welfare "loafers," while gargantuan military budgets went unquestioned.

Contrary to the impression that public assistance creates a permanent underclass of welfare "loafers" who live in comfort without having to work, 80 percent of welfare recipients receive benefits for only two years and 50 percent are off welfare within one year. Most who apply for welfare do so reluctantly: because they were forced to by a precipitous loss of income due to illness, death or desertion by the person who had provided the income for the family. Women with dependent children go on welfare because their husbands lose their jobs or desert them or they are forced to flee an abusive relationship and they themselves are unemployed. They use welfare to tide themselves over while they look for a job or the skills to acquire one. The high costs of child care prevent many from getting training and taking jobs.

Although the federal government sets an official poverty level, each state sets the percentage of that level they will pay in aid. On average, this amounts to only 50 percent of poverty level and for some states, such as Mississippi, far less than that. AFDC grants often are barely enough to pay for housing, and recipients depend on putting together aid from several programs, such as food stamps, to meet basic needs. Recipients of aid cannot have assets of more than $1,000 and often are not allowed to own personal property, such as a car, that is worth more than a few hundred dollars. That means high maintenance costs for an old car, rather than a newer car that is less costly to maintain. Because many cannot get to jobs or job-training programs without a car, such requirements are counterproductive.

Those who get jobs that pay less than their assistance have nevertheless had their assistance proportionally reduced and have lost Medicaid and food stamps. Also, many states give aid only to a family without a "man in the house," even though he may be unemployed. These regulations act as disincentives to work or to keep families intact, yet these women are blamed for not working and not having husbands. The same persons who cry out against

52

When May 1, 1938, found Ohio's relief funds gone, clients lined up for blocks before the Cleveland Relief Bureau for "surplus" food. Photo courtesy of the Social Welfare History Archives, University of Minnesota.

women having too many children on welfare also make family-planning assistance unavailable to them.

The reasons welfare doesn't work lie in these meager levels of aid and the punitive regulations built into the system — not because those receiving aid are not seeking the education and the

WELFARE MYTHS

Only one out of four recipients is totally dependent on AFDC (and supplementary public assistance programs such as Food Stamps) for their family's income. In contrast, three out of four "package" AFDC income with earnings from their own employment, with the earnings and benefits of other family members (including child support), and with other resources. Those who do package income sources are more likely to escape poverty — six out of 10 who package income from AFDC, their own earnings, and the income of other family members, manage to bring their family's income to the poverty line.

Excerpted from the testimony of Roberta Spalter-Roth, Director of Research, Institute for Women's Policy Research, before the Subcommittee on Human Resources of the House Ways and Means Committee, February 2, 1995.

training to become self-supportive.

Those who have studied the system from the perspective of the needs of recipients have recommended a number of reforms. These include Head Start programs available for all low-income children, job training that really prepares people for existing jobs and helps them find such jobs, child-care services to those working or in educational and training programs, family-planning help, the right to combine public assistance with income from work until the poverty level is reached — $11,570 for a family of three — and the right to maintain intact families on public assistance, as well as job-training programs for fathers.

Unfortunately, most of the "reforms" being discussed are aimed more at further punishing the poor and pushing as many off assistance as soon as possible. This includes "workfare" in place of welfare (getting the same low grant but now in exchange for working at a dead-end job), cutting off all teenage mothers, as well as recent immigrants. Many states are considering programs in which a recipient must be in job training, and the programs are cut off in two years, whether or not they have a job, but there is little provision that the job training will be meaningfully related to getting a job or that affordable child care will be available to preschool children.

CORPORATE WELFARE

As congressional Republicans targeted the school lunch program, food stamps and aid to unwed mothers, Shapiro and libertarian counterparts at the Cato Institute joined to take on corporate welfare — the $100-billion-a-year treasure chest of subsidies, tax breaks and special deals for U.S. businesses.

Robert Shapiro proposed scaling back farm price-supports, government-subsidized electricity, tax breaks for the oil industry and (sorry, Boss) newspaper advertisers over five years. That would save a total of $265 billion. Stephen Moore of Republican-friendly Cato was more radical. Zero out all corporate welfare, he said, "and we could cut the federal deficit in half."

Lars-Erik Nelson, "Ending Corporate Welfare Would Benefit Everyone," **Newsday**, March, 1995. (Robert Shapiro is an economist at the Progressive Policy Institute.)

These plans show that the power holders in America continue to view poor women alone with children as deviants who deserve to be punished, rather than people with rights to dignity and basic necessities. A social and economic system that pays women poorly, assumes that they are normatively dependent on a husband's income and regards them as the primary child-carers regularly drops women out of the bottom of that system as poor heads of households and then victimizes them again by condemning them as responsible for their plights.

WELFARE: A MAN'S PERSPECTIVE

Ronald K. Henry

Ronald K. Henry presented the following testimony on behalf of the Men's Health Network to the Subcommittee on Human Resources.

■ POINTS TO CONSIDER

1. Restate the greatest causal factor in family breakdown.

2. Discuss the role of fathers in the welfare system.

3. Summarize the four areas of Henry's welfare reform.

4. Which area do you think is most important?

Excerpted from the testimony of Ronald K. Henry before the Subcommittee on Human Resources of the House Ways and Means Committee, February 2, 1995.

Fathers are the immunization program that reduce the tragic need for bandaids and tonics.

Virtually all of our social welfare programs are bandaids and tonics to treat our childrens' afflictions. Fathers are the immunization program that reduce the tragic need for bandaids and tonics. Too often, our government programs have forgotten the simple axiom that prevention is better than treatment. This hearing on welfare reform specifically demonstrates the need to reform government programs that focus on treating symptoms while leaving the cause of the symptoms in place.

In virtually all of our programs, the phrase "family preservation" has become narrowly defined to mean the propping up of the single mother household as a stand-alone entity. While most single parents do all they can for their children, and many children of single parents develop beautifully, the inescapable history of our programs demonstrates that many single-mother households will never succeed as stand-alone units and many children in those households are in grave danger, both physically and developmentally.

The tunnel vision that afflicts current "family preservation" efforts can be seen at all stages of the child welfare process. It is rare for a caseworker even to seek the identity of the child's father and almost unheard of for the caseworker to seek information regarding the father's fitness and willingness to provide for the child's needs. If the father independently comes forward in an effort to assist the child, the caseworker's standard response is to resist all involvement other than cash transfer payments. This resistance is wrong. The government's interest is in protecting the child and not in defending one parent's ownership of that child against all others. "Family preservation" must be understood to include and encourage the participation of fathers and must move beyond the mere administration of programs designed to prop up the single parent as a stand-alone entity.

The absurdity of the current system is even more starkly highlighted in situations where the caseworker realizes that the child must be taken from the care of the single mother. In every state in the country, the standard operating procedure is for the bureaucracy to skip over the father and the entire extended family and consider only third party placement. The bureaucracy's fallacy is in viewing child placement as a simple dichotomy — an unfit single mother versus third-party foster care or adoption.

It is time to reform welfare. We must change the systems under which our only criteria are that beneficiaries must continue to neither work nor marry. Children are harmed when the unintended consequence of policy is to favor non-working, single-parent households over all others.

OVERVIEW OF PRINCIPLES AND PROGRAMS

There is widespread agreement that the current welfare system is destructive of the families it was intended to help. Despite its good intentions, the government has made a devil's bargain with the poor — "We will give you money as long as you continue to neither work nor marry." Current programs and many reform proposals are patronizing. They assume that large classes of citizens are simply too stupid and incompetent to make any current or near term contribution to their own support. Real welfare reform requires recognition that there is no respect for the individual unless there is respect for the individual's labor.

1. "Making Work Pay": Rhetoric and Reality

Work always pays. Our problem is that we have established a parallel system under which non-work often pays better. Most law-abiding citizens work 40 or 45 years to qualify for a social security benefit that is smaller than a teenager's welfare package. Many welfare recipients are not unemployed, they are prematurely retired. Welfare reform requires attention to four areas: *responsibility, paternity, accountability,* and *eligibility.*

2. Responsibility

Responsibility should be immediate, mandatory and universal. Beginning immediately with entry into any welfare program, every recipient should be required to devote 40 hours per week to some combination of job search, training and work, with a strong emphasis on work. Actual work experience is generally the best training for advancement in the work place. An immediate, universal work requirement also eliminates the "no job" option and encourages serious search efforts for the best available job.

3. Paternity

Current policy fails to distinguish between "runaway" and "thrown away" or "driven away" parents. The federal government spends approximately two billion dollars per year on child support enforcement but purposefully and consciously excludes

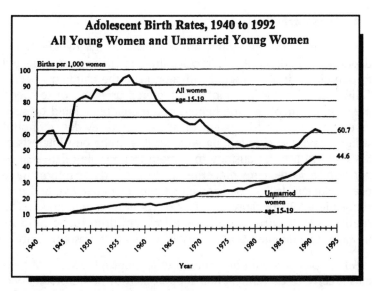

Adolescent Birth Rates, 1940 to 1992
All Young Women and Unmarried Young Women

Births per 1,000 women

All women
age 15-19

60.7

44.6

Unmarried
women
age 15-19

Year

Source: Congressional Reference Service.

fathers from all parent-child programs. Under current AFDC rules, the low-income father who wishes to be a physical and emotional asset to his children also becomes a financial liability by disqualifying them from most assistance. Research conducted by Health and Human Services (HHS) itself confirms that both mothers and fathers distrust the bureaucracy and work jointly to conceal paternity. We cannot be surprised by low-income parents who separate or conceal paternity when our policies make such behavior the economically ration-al course. A work requirement for single parents and an end to discrimination against two-parent households will change the dynamics of paternity establishment.

Eligibility for all federal programs should require establishment of paternity, beginning with eligibility for the WIC program. That program itself must be revised to develop and encourage the roles of fathers. Paternity establishment forms in hospital programs should encourage the parties to voluntarily establish custody and visitation as well as financial support. Avoidance of poverty and welfare dependency are directly linked to father involvement. Child support compliance exceeds 90 percent in joint custody families. Child poverty rates and welfare dependency rates are much lower in father-custody families than in mother-custody. Women's workforce participation and economic security are increased in joint custody and father-custody families.

4. Accountability

AFDC and other programs are intended for the benefit of the dependent children. Adults receive the benefits and are expected to participate in the programs in support of the children's needs. Failure or refusal to participate in required programs or to spend the cash payments for the benefit of the children should be seen as evidence of child neglect or abuse. Such evidence should weigh heavily in determining whether it is in the best interests of the child to transfer custody to a more responsible relative or to consider a foster care placement. Prior efforts at reform have been reluctant to impose sanctions upon uncooperative and irresponsible adults because of a fear of "punishing the child." The reality is that current policies allow children to be held as hostages to guarantee continued subsidy of adult irresponsibility.

All recipients should be required to reimburse the value of benefits received. Currently, child support paid by non-custodial parents is used for reimbursement after a $50 per month waiver. The custodial parent should have the obligation to reimburse one-half of the welfare payments made on behalf of the child and each adult should have the obligation to reimburse benefits paid on behalf of that adult. Many welfare recipients require only short term assistance and that assistance can fairly be treated as a loan or a line of credit rather than as a grant. A uniform reimbursement requirement also encourages all recipients to minimize the period of dependency, take no more benefits than are required, and resume paid employment at the earliest possible date. Community service should be counted toward the reimbursement obligation but should be valued at a level that does not compete with the attractiveness of paid employment.

5. Eligibility

Under the law of each state, parents have an obligation of financial responsibility for their minor children. If the minor children themselves become parents, the minor parents should continue to be the obligation of their own parents. Accordingly, the birth of a child to minor parents may create a requirement for welfare assistance to the new infant but does not create a requirement for assistance to the minor parents unless their own parents are unable to supply the required support. Minor parents must live with or at the expense of their own parents. Payments on behalf of the new infant should be made to the parents of the minor parents as their guardians.

CRADLE-TO-GRAVE WELFARE

Addressing what is perhaps the central provision of the Contract with America, the Republican-controlled House launched the first serious legislative assault on one of the most pernicious social experiments in American history — the cradle-to-grave federal welfare system. Particularly over the last three decades, that system — whose underlying premise is that human beings cannot be held responsible for their own actions — has undermined the American family, marginalized traditional religious organizations and private charitable institutions, decimated true community, and turned the nation's cities into vast pockets of despair, violence, and squalor.

"Should U.S. Taxpayers Subsidize Illegitimacy: Catholic Bishops Say Yes," **Human Events**, 31 March, 1995: 1.

Welfare payments should be limited to citizens and immigrants with refugee status. Income-based eligibility standards should consider both the income of the parents and any resources that are voluntarily available from the kinship network.

WELFARE: A WOMAN'S PERSPECTIVE

Cynthia I. Newbille

Cynthia I. Newbille is executive director of the National Black Women's Health Project. NBWHP is a national self-help and health advocacy organization committed to the empowerment of Black women through wellness education.

■ POINTS TO CONSIDER

1. Why is a minimum wage increase included in the author's proposals for welfare reform?

2. Discuss why effective welfare reform cannot be accomplished without universal health care.

3. How is the problem of employment related to welfare reform?

4. Contrast the approach to welfare reform in the previous reading to that of NBWHP.

Excerpted from the statement of Cynthia I. Newbille before the Subcommittee on Human Resources of the House Ways and Means Committee, February 2, 1995.

Welfare reform legislation cannot be accomplished without universal health care.

The National Black Women's Health Project (NBWHP) believes that in order to move low-income people out of poverty, a complete overhaul of the welfare system is necessary. We would make the following suggestions for comprehensive reform:

Comprehensive Job Creation Strategy

The main objective of welfare reform should be to facilitate the movement of low-income families from a system that perpetuates a lifelong cycle of dependency on government benefits. A commitment by Congress to enact welfare reform legislation that provides employment for those who want to work, is a first step towards ensuring that welfare recipients break the cycle of dependency. A comprehensive job creation strategy is necessary to accomplish this goal.

Congress must acknowledge its acceptance of a consistent targeted national unemployment rate of 6% (13 million unemployed). In doing so, Members must assess the impact of this implicit policy target on the ability of all people to find employment. As a first step in addressing this issue, welfare reform must promote the principles of full employment. It should include a comprehensive program to ensure that there is a job for everyone who wants a job. A comprehensive job creation strategy must ensure that jobs provide liveable wages.

States should be given economic incentives to develop programs that will enable welfare recipients to move into public/private sector jobs without government coercion. The use of tax breaks or partial wage subsidies can be used as an incentive for employers to provide employment to welfare recipients. In addition, low income working families (at or below the federal poverty level) must be allowed continued receipt of benefits such as food stamps and Medicaid.

Raising the National Minimum Wage

True welfare reform must promote self-sufficiency and independence. Congress must raise the national minimum wage as part of the strategy for reform. The inability to find employment that provides a liveable wage is the primary reason cited by low-income families who have temporarily received welfare benefits. Raising the minimum wage to an appropriate level, adjusting yearly for inflation, would be a significant step towards securing economic independence for low income families.

Continued expansion of the Earned Income Tax Credit (EITC) would also help to increase the wages of low-income workers. The EITC allows workers to receive an advance credit of up to 60%. The expanded EITC raises a minimum wage job ($4.25 per hour to $6.00 per hour) for an employee with two or more children.

Universal Health Care Reform

Welfare reform legislation cannot be accomplished without universal health care. Many welfare recipients are trapped in a system of dependency because they cannot find employment that provides health care benefits for their families. Universal health care coverage for families will enable recipients to leave the welfare system without the fear of losing health coverage for their families.

Newly employed welfare recipients must have continued coverage under the Medicaid Program. In addition, the working poor must have access to health care coverage. A good first step toward increasing coverage for the working poor under incremental reform legislation would include phased-in employer mandates.

Housing

Adequate housing, rent subsidies and standard public housing must be an integrated part of comprehensive welfare reform. Demonstration programs must be provided that allow for community involvement. Programs which allow families to move into "mainstream" housing or apartment units through housing or rent vouchers must be given priority. In addition, every effort must be made to increase the availability of public housing for low-income families.

Education/Training

States must be given the necessary resources to provide welfare recipients with educational opportunities and job training. These services, however, must not be prerequisites for receiving welfare benefits. Educational opportunities should include post-secondary education (college) or vocational training which place an emphasis

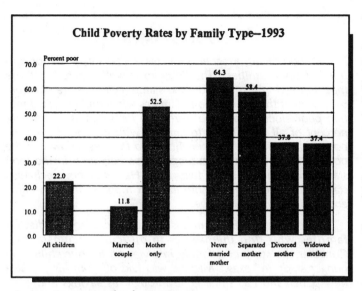

Child Poverty Rates by Family Type—1993

Source: Congressional Reference Service.

on the development of skills. This will help recipients achieve independence and self-sufficiency rather than temporary employment.

Child Care

Comprehensive welfare reform legislation must include child care. Funding for child care is necessary for the working poor to help them stay self-sufficient. Lack of child care or money for child care is often a major impediment for the working poor. The same holds true for families when leaving the welfare system. Since child care costs are often higher than a family's take home pay, many families are often economically worse off paying for child care when employed than under the welfare system.

Currently, welfare recipients enrolled in the JOBS Program receive child care while working, in training programs or when enrolled in school. They also receive child care for up to one year after leaving welfare for employment. In order to help move families out of the welfare system, the provision of child care should be mandatory for all welfare recipients. Also, the promotion of child care in the workplace and within the public school system should be a top priority. States must receive additional funding to provide these services.

FOOD STAMPS

The Food Stamp Program provides a vital safety net for millions of poor families. The Program is well-targeted to those most in need. Over 50% of food stamp recipients are children; over 80% of the benefits go to families with children. Two million poor elderly persons also receive food stamps. About 97 percent of all benefits go to families with incomes below the poverty line; 56% of the benefits go to families below half the poverty line. The average length of participation in the food stamp program is less than two years. Half of all new recipients stay on the program no more than six months, and two-thirds end participation within a year.

The Food Stamp Program ensures a basic adequate diet for families who find themselves in difficult circumstances. Consider the story of a family interviewed for our childhood hunger study in Texas. Michael was laid off from his job at a newspaper and has since gone through his savings and even sold some possessions in order to provide for himself, his wife and their three children. Michael now receives food stamps to help him provide adequate food for his kids. Without food stamps, Michael says, the family could be out on the street.

Thousands of families across the country have told us similar stories — stories of how food stamps make the difference between having enough food and being hungry.

The Food Stamp Program works for these families because it is able to respond at times when the need is the greatest. During a recession, food stamp participation increases; when the economy improves, food stamp participation drops. For example, between June 1990 and June 1992, as the national unemployment rate increased from 5.1% to 7.7%, food stamp participation increased by more than 5 million. Now, as the economy strengthens, participation is steadily decreasing.

The Food Stamp Program also acts as an equalizer — assuring that families receive adequate food no matter what state they live in. There are currently enormous disparities in AFDC benefits from state to state that cannot be explained by differences in the cost of living. Since food stamp benefits vary with income, they are low in states with high AFDC payments, while in states with low AFDC payments, the Food Stamp Program's federal dollars make up the difference.

Excerpted from the testimony of Robert J. Fersh, President, Food Research and Action Center, before the Subcommittee on Human Resources of the House Ways and Means Committee, February 2, 1995.

Child Support Enhancement

Mandatory paternity establishment before receipt of welfare benefits is not an effective mechanism to provide support for poor women and their families. Welfare benefits should not be linked to paternity establishment.

The amount of child support awards must be increased to reflect the needs of families. Stricter child support enforcement guidelines are also necessary under reform. Federal requirements which mandate the revocation of professional licenses and enforcement of child support orders and awards may help in the collection of some payments. However, in Black communities that are already overburdened with high unemployment levels, this could prove to be ineffective.

Family Support

Welfare reform legislation should place an emphasis on improving the quality of life for families. Support programs such as parenting classes, nutrition and substance abuse programs and the elimination of policies which penalize two-parent households must be included in any proposal enacted by Congress.

Legislators have attempted to address welfare reform issues for the past 60 years. In those 60 years of failed social experiments on the poor, welfare recipients have rarely been asked what they need. There is no magic solution for poverty, unemployment or welfare dependency. However, as a first step, Members of Congress must recognize the true problems of the welfare system. Most of our recommendations for welfare reform legislation may not be politically popular or expedient, but they must be seriously considered as suggestions to current legislative proposals.

READING

8

WORKFARE TO END WELFARE: THE POINT

Jeffrey H. Joseph

Jeffrey H. Joseph presented the following statement to the Senate Finance Committee on behalf of the U.S. Chamber of Commerce. The Chamber is the world's largest federation of business associations and is the principle spokesperson for the American business community, representing more than 220,000 businesses and organizations.

■ POINTS TO CONSIDER

1. Give examples of how government and the private sector can work together for welfare reform.

2. List some of the core proposals of the Chamber for welfare-to-work.

3. Discuss the disincentives employers encounter in hiring welfare recipients.

4. What place do drugs and alcohol have in the workfare discussion?

Excerpted from the statement of the U.S. Chamber of Commerce before the Senate Finance Committee, March 20, 1995.

The Chamber believes that welfare recipients can effectively contribute to American productivity.

The U.S. Chamber of Commerce, representing 220,000 businesses, 3,000 state and local chambers of commerce, 1,200 trade and professional associations, and 72 American Chambers of Commerce abroad, commends the Senate Committee on Finance for recognizing the importance of welfare reform and its implications for our nation's economic and social well-being. The Chamber also appreciates this opportunity to present the business community's views on this critical issue. We are deeply committed to working with members of Congress to promote meaningful welfare reform during the 104th Congress.

The nation's welfare system is in dire need of restructuring. Welfare has become a system that today creates dependence rather than self-sufficiency. The business community has long advocated "welfare-to-work" as a positive option for reforming this system. We are encouraged that this position has emerged as a consensus. Structurally, current proposals focus on moving primary responsibility for welfare programs to the states in the form of block grants. The Chamber supports increased state and local flexibility in the delivery of federal programs.

PROPOSALS

Welfare reform proposals under consideration will limit the amount and/or duration of benefits and require set percentages of able-bodied recipients to obtain employment over time. The Chamber supports time limits and a work requirement for those on the welfare rolls. We anticipate that the business community will be called upon to provide that employment. Therefore, it is essential that business be involved in the design, development, operation, and evaluation of any changes in America's welfare system.

Chamber members place a high priority on reforming welfare. In a recent survey to construct the Chamber's National Business Agenda, welfare reform was second (behind unfunded mandates) on a list of 64 issues ranked by importance to members. Last fall, the Chamber surveyed 1,200 of its members to determine their specific interests in welfare reform. Ninety-nine percent of the survey respondents advocate an overhaul of the current welfare system. While 76 percent say that welfare recipients should be eligible for federally funded education and training, 98 percent believe that those who receive such services should be required to work. An overwhelming percentage — 94 percent — support placing a limit on the amount of time that one can receive welfare benefits.

COMPREHENSIVE REFORM

Comprehensive welfare reform is a complex issue with many human and economic dimensions. Our piece of the puzzle is focused on selective and critical issues from the perspective of workplace employment: (1) workers must have the knowledge, skills, and attitudes to enter and succeed in the workplace; and (2) some employers may need incentives to hire such workers, while others may require the removal of disincentives that may make job creation prohibitively expensive or expose employers to unnecessary legal risk.

For these reasons, the Chamber is deeply committed to working with Congress to enact sound welfare reform policy. Specifically, the U.S. Chamber Board of Directors recently approved the following as broad policy guidelines:

1. Focus national attention on measures to ensure that welfare recipients will be equipped with the knowledge, skills, and attitudes needed to obtain and retain jobs in the private or public sectors.

2. Devise incentives — such as tax incentives, training grants, or establishment of realistic local marketplace training wages — for employers to move people from welfare to work. Consider also temporarily waiving provisions of statutes that may serve as dis-incentives for employers to hire welfare recipients.

3. Include provisions to ensure that welfare recipients will be drug- and alcohol-free as a condition of receiving welfare benefits and other forms of federal assistance.

4. Consider welfare-to-work reform in the context of the elements of a locally driven workforce development system and reliable labor market information. For example, from the employers' perspective, consider how placing welfare recipients in jobs balances with moving others into the workplace — young people from school-to-work, dislocated workers transitioning from career to career, and others — in a climate where employers are restructuring to compete in a global environment.

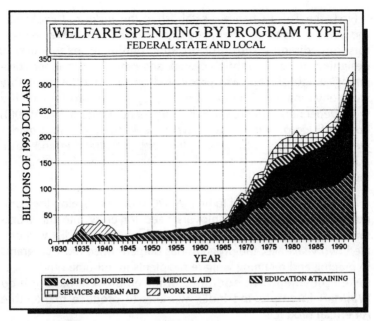

WELFARE SPENDING BY PROGRAM TYPE
FEDERAL STATE AND LOCAL

BILLIONS OF 1993 DOLLARS

YEAR

CASH FOOD HOUSING   MEDICAL AID   EDUCATION &TRAINING
SERVICES &URBAN AID   WORK RELIEF

Source: Heritage Foundation in Congressional testimony by Robert Rector, March 9, 1995.

The complexities of the global marketplace and the rapid progression of today's knowledge-based economy realistically should focus on welfare-to-work strategies, including ladders to high-skill, high-wage jobs. Whether being prepared for entry-level employment in the low-tech service industry or as a high-tech toolmaker apprentice, consideration must be given to how best to prepare welfare recipients with basic skills, attitudes, and work ethics that employers demand.

COMMUNITY MODELS

Two interesting community models have shown encouraging results with the added dimension of creating new jobs in their respective communities and moving people from welfare-to-work. One example is in Tulsa, Oklahoma. The Tulsa Chamber of Commerce was approached by one of its members, which is a major supplier to WalMart. WalMart's desire to market products made in America resulted in its assertion that additional product lines would in fact be carried by WalMart, if its supplier could find U.S. workers to produce this particular product — fishing rods — which were not being made in America.

First, the Tulsa Chamber established the *Industrial Exchange, Inc. (IndEx) Program*. Then, key Chamber officials tackled regulatory impediments and built on their significant experience in designing successful school-to-work and other job placement programs. Establishment was predicated on relaxing the regulatory work environment. The partnership program for Aid for Families with Dependent Children (AFDC) mothers operates as a 501(c)(3) non-profit corporation. Five days a week, the program provides welfare recipients with pre-employment skills training and basic skills education as well as work experience in manufacturing fishing rods.

All training is designed to help AFDC mothers develop the competencies which local employers need for entry into the workforce. Employees are paid $9-$10 per hour. Since IndEx was created two years ago, the program has outperformed most programs in placing and retaining welfare recipients in full-time private-sector employment. In addition, other employers have joined WalMart in employing IndEx workers to produce marketable American products.

In Michigan, *Focus: Hope* has established a number of intensive workplace training experiences for young adults to gain industry standards of discipline, productivity, and personal conduct as they improve academic and communications skills, learn computer applications, and develop technical career options in manufacturing. To qualify for the program, applicants must perform math and reading at a minimum eighth-grade level and be drug-free. There are no other prerequisites. Thousands of people have moved through this program and have been placed in jobs paying $7 to $12 per hour. Achieving starting income levels in this range may provide adequate financial incentives for participants to move off of welfare.

The Oklahoma and Michigan examples reflect real local employment needs which begs the notion that this debate might most productively be framed "from the jobs backward." Every community needs to develop a strategy with a major emphasis on its human capital capabilities for its own economic self-sufficiency. Governors and trade delegations are travelling the globe every day trying to lure world-class employers to their states and communities. For this reason, the welfare-to-work strategy must be incorporated into a community's comprehensive human capital strategy.

INCOME MAINTENANCE

Ever since the New Deal, which set the framework for the United States transfer payment systems, U.S. anti-poverty efforts have focused on income maintenance and social service provision. The limits of this approach are becoming clear: the income maintenance system has become a sort of economic methadone which eases the pain of poverty and unemployment but does not address the underlying causes. Worse, if unintentionally, the current system actually penalizes poor families who attempt to move forward through education, work or self employment.

Excerpted from the testimony of Robert E. Friedman and Cicero Wilson, Corporation for Enterprise Development, before the Senate Finance Committee, March 20, 1995.

CONCLUSION

The Chamber firmly believes that welfare recipients — as other potential employees — must have drug-free status as a condition of employment and be familiar with the responsibilities associated with drug-free workplace policies and programs. It is estimated that substance abuse and its consequences cost the economy an estimated $180 to $250 billion annually. Surveys show that substance abuse is viewed as a major problem by 88 percent of all U.S. companies. A drug-free workforce is essential to successful enterprise.

If American industry is to be competitive, and if our national economy is to become stronger, we absolutely must have a competitive workforce. The Chamber believes that welfare recipients can effectively contribute to American productivity. By considering the issues I have outlined today, the nation can move closer to achieving what has been attempted for many decades — reforming America's welfare system and providing opportunities for recipients to enter and sustain a lifetime of independence and earning. The U.S. Chamber of Commerce stands ready to assist Congress, states, and communities in this most critical endeavor.

READING

9

WORKFARE TO END WELFARE: THE COUNTERPOINT

Barbara R. Bergmann and Heidi I. Hartmann

Barbara R. Bergmann is a Professor of Economics at American University, Washington, D.C. Heidi I. Hartmann is founder and president of the Institute for Women's Policy Research.

■ **POINTS TO CONSIDER**

1. What issues has the welfare debate avoided, according to the authors?

2. Discuss the potential impact on unemployment of an additional 2.5 million single mothers entering the labor force.

3. How can the government help finance workfare programs?

4. Summarize two essential proposals necessary to help single mothers enter the labor force at low-skill positions.

Barbara Bergmann and Heidi Hartmann, "A Program to Help Working Parents," **The Nation**, 1 May 1995: 592-95. Reprinted with permission from **The Nation** magazine. ©The Nation Company, L.P.

The Help for Working Parents program could be financed by shifting funds from the many now-superfluous defense programs, the C.I.A., military aid to foreign governments and agricultural payments to wealthy farmers.

In the wake of defeats on the issues of term limits and the balanced budget amendment, Republican hopes of glory from the Contract with America depend heavily on welfare legislation. Yet the welfare bill the Republican House has passed is not in any sense a reform. It does nothing at all to promote what both Republicans and Democrats say is a major goal — getting single mothers to make the transition from welfare to a job. Real reform would address the problems that keep many single mothers from being able to leave welfare, and it would require substantial new spending.

DYSFUNCTIONAL SYSTEM

The fact is that the welfare system, dysfunctional as it currently is, was invented to take care of a real problem: There are single mothers who need help because they cannot earn enough to cover the minimal needs of their families. Even if it were true that without welfare there would be fewer out-of-wedlock children, those children are here, and they cannot be allowed to starve. They cannot be supported by the Kiwanis Club, as the Republican Governor of Virginia recently suggested. Nor will the American people find it in their hearts to make mothers so desperate as to give up their children to orphanages, in order that the pitiful sight might deter other poor women from new pregnancies.

The Republicans know that. Their alternative, sending the whole mess back to the states accompanied by block grants, is basically a retreat from their "cut 'em off" rhetoric to a far less generous version of the present system. Pretty much the same people will be on welfare, but each family will get less, pushing them deeper into poverty. As the states compete through low taxes to attract industry and well-off residents, state-controlled programs helping poor children will get still more stingy. President Clinton's proposed reform appears to be one more of those unsatisfactory compromises to which he is prone, an attempt to graft a modest amount of "cut 'em off" onto the present badly flawed system.

Since government must help some parents with some of the expenses of raising their children, we must consider whether there is a better alternative to current proposals that could get a higher proportion of single parents into jobs and reduce the number of improvident births, but that would also lower the proportion of children in poverty instead of raising it as the Republican plans threaten to do.

This more humane approach would guarantee help for working parents that would make jobs more attractive than welfare. Currently, mothers on A.F.D.C. get their health insurance and child care needs met; if they leave welfare for full-time jobs, they usually have to pay those expenses by themselves. Many have to settle for jobs without basic health benefits, and don't have relatives who can supply good, safe, full-time child care for free. Most single mothers on welfare cannot earn enough to pay for decent shelter and other necessities if they also have to pay out of their wages for child care and health insurance.

HEALTH CARE

If the costs of health care and child care were covered, even a minimum-wage full-time job would provide enough for a family consisting of a mother and two children to live at a decent standard, assuming it was supplemented by food stamps and the earned-income tax credit at levels allowed by current law, and by help with housing in high-rent areas. With that kind of assistance, plus more aid in collecting child support, women in jobs would be far better off than those on welfare. That would powerfully increase the incentive to leave welfare for a job, and many current welfare recipients would try to do so. Our proposal, which we call *Help for Working Parents,* would feature government help with health insurance and child care to families with children — not just as a transition when families leave welfare but for as long as they need the services. Benefits would be available to parents who had never been on welfare, and to married parents as well as single ones. And there would be a beneficial side effect — women with jobs want fewer children than women who stay home, and in fact they have fewer.

If providing health care and child care to poor women has the effects we anticipate, many of the single mothers now on A.F.D.C. will seek jobs and actually find them. Administration officials seem to believe they would not be fit to hold any jobs without

EXPLOITATION

The real purpose of the G.O.P.'s attack on welfare is not to improve an admittedly flawed program but to advance a broader conservative agenda...An immediate goal of the right is to insure a continuing supply of employees for the low-wage service industries and factory sweatshops, which depend on a non-unionized, disproportionately female work force. These women will be even more vulnerable to exploitation under the proposed legislation. This pressure will be applied by a welfare bureaucracy, whose job will be to require welfare mothers to accept the unappetizing employment choices they are given, at the risk of losing support for themselves and their children. We already have a flourishing system of coercive treatment of young black men, who are in prison or on parole in record numbers; welfare reform will complete the circle.

Sumner M. Rosen, "The True End of Welfare Reform," **The Nation**, 3 April, 1995: 456.

elaborate, expensive and time-consuming training. Many liberals also assume that there are no jobs for them to fit into. Both of these assumptions can be challenged.

Teenagers get and perform satisfactorily in low-skill jobs by the millions without being enrolled in training to make them "job-ready." Many single parents have high school diplomas and some work experience. There is no reason to think that single parents in general are grossly inferior as workers to average teenagers. Some single mothers will continue to be out of a job whatever policy we adopt. Some are disabled, and some are caring for disabled children. Some have drug or alcohol problems. There will be some who lose their jobs and need support while finding others. The *Help for Working Parents* program would have to be supplemented with fallback aid for such people, perhaps with benefits mostly in the form of vouchers.

LABOR FORCE

Those who argue that welfare can never be reformed because there are not enough jobs available make the patently wrong assumption that new entrants into the labor force must endure unemployment until the number of jobs grows to accommodate them. In fact, there is considerable turnover, particularly in low-wage jobs, and new entrants compete with those previously in the labor force for the vacancies that result. At worst, assuming no increase at all in the number of jobs, the addition of 2.5 million single mothers to the labor force might raise the unemployment rate by less than two points. In fact, there would be many new jobs in child care centers and an increase in employment in industries supplying additional consumer goods to the new workers. In areas with high unemployment rates, some public-service jobs might have to be created.

The cost of a *Help for Working Parents* program would depend on how many welfare clients become employed. We estimate that the program would cost about $90 billion a year in new spending, most of it for child care and health care services. Of that amount, 60 percent would go to provide vouchers for licensed child care for preschool children and after-school care for older children. Care would be provided free to families in the bottom 20 percent, and at sliding-scale fees to middle-class families. This program would provide some help with child care expenses to 60 percent of American families with children. Some of the funds would go to convert half-day kindergarten and Head Start programs, which now offer little help to working parents, into full-day programs. These facilities would provide children with a safe environment, get them ready for school and diagnose and treat their physical and emotional problems.

The rest of the money would provide health insurance to all nine million uninsured children and the adults in their families. If a program of universal health insurance coverage had passed last year, this would not be considered part of the price of welfare reform, but under current conditions it must be.

The *Help for Working Parents* proposal is broadly similar to a set of successful programs in France. The French government provides free high-quality all-day nursery school for all children between 2 1/2 and 6, and subsidizes care for infants and toddlers. It offers health insurance for all and family allowances to parents, whether single or married. As a result only 25 percent of French single mothers stay home on an A.F.D.C.-type program; the comparable U.S. figure is 32 percent higher. And only 6 percent of French children are poor, compared with 23 percent of American children.

78

The *Help for Working Parents* program could be financed by shifting funds from the many now-superfluous defense programs, the C.I.A., military aid to foreign governments and agricultural payments to wealthy farmers. It will not, of course, happen under the current Republican ascendancy, nor while the mania against government continues to rage. But discussing this proposal now will put it on the agenda for the day when the opposition to the right wing again finds its voice, and when the public recognizes once more the need for government to help with problems that the market causes or cannot solve.

READING

10

GOVERNMENT WELFARE CORRUPTS THE POOR

John Ashcroft

John Ashcroft is a Republican representing Missouri in the United States Senate.

■ POINTS TO CONSIDER

1. Summarize the analogy between colonialism and welfare.

2. Why does Ashcroft feel the war on poverty has failed?

3. Discuss what Ashcroft believes are the basic goals of welfare.

4. What policy measures does the author advocate?

John Ashcroft, "The De-Colonization of Welfare," delivered before the Northeast Republican Leadership Conference, May 21, 1995. Reprinted with permission of **Vital Speeches**.

What our Washington-based welfare system has done, particularly to women and children, has been to fashion a new form of colonialism.

Thirty years ago, the great movement reshaping world politics was the end of colonialism. John Kennedy celebrated the "desire to be independent," as the "single most important force in the world." Eventually this movement revealed its power from Asia to Africa to South America.

The problem with imperialism was not just its economic exploitation. It was its influence on culture. It undermined traditional ways and institutions. It was inconsistent with human dignity. Why? Because imperialism rewarded passivity and encouraged dependence. It required citizens to live by the rules of a distant elite. It demanded people be docile in the face of a system that they could not change. It was an attack, not just on national sovereignty, but on national character.

What our Washington-based welfare system has done, particularly to women and children, has been to fashion a new form of colonialism. It creates an underclass that is paid to play by rules that lead to dependence. It rewards behavior that keeps them powerless. It thwarts the efforts of private and religious charitable organizations to care for the needy. It discourages the genuine compassion of the American people. It has waged war against the human spirit.

RENEWING DIGNITY

Our goal in welfare should not be to maintain the "underclass" as comfortably as possible as wards of the state. Yet that is precisely what has been done. Cash benefits anesthetize their suffering. Food Stamps relieve their hunger. Health care and housing are provided. But the hope, dignity, and integrity of independence are forgotten.

Consider, just briefly, what our current welfare system has wrought. The numbers alone are enough to numb the senses. Since 1965, we've spent more than $5 trillion — a cost higher than that of waging the Second World War — fighting poverty. Yet today, there are more people living in poverty than ever before, and our safety net has become more like quicksand.

In 1965, when President Johnson launched the "war on poverty," there were approximately 14.7 million children in poverty. They constituted about one of every five children in America. In 1993, there were 14.6 million children in poverty. They constitute a little more than one in every five American children. Of all age groups, children are the most likely to be poor. In 1991, a study of the poverty rates in eight industrialized nations revealed that American children were almost three times as likely to be poor as children from the other nations studied.

The character of the poverty we face today is a deeper, more entrenched poverty in which generations of people are born, live, and die without the experience of holding a job, owning a home, or growing up with a father's love and discipline. Go into our inner-cities and you will meet a generation fed on welfare and food stamps but starved of nurture and hope. You will meet young teens in their third pregnancy. You will meet children who are not only without a father, but don't know anyone who has a father. You will talk with sixth-graders who don't know how many inches are in a foot, having never seen a ruler, and with first-graders who don't know their ABCs or numbers because no one ever took the time to teach them.

Thirty years ago, Robert Kennedy reflected on welfare and said this, "Opponents of welfare have always said that welfare is degrading, both to the giver and the recipient. They have said that it destroys self-respect, that it lowers incentive, that it is contrary to American ideals. Most of us deprecated and disregarded these criticisms. People were in need; obviously, we felt, to help people in trouble was the right thing to do. But in our urge to help, we also disregarded elementary fact. For the criticisms of welfare do have a center of truth, and they are confirmed by the evidence."

Robert Kennedy's warnings were not heeded.

WINNING THE WAR ON POVERTY

The political elites that followed him have spent, and taxed, and redistributed wealth beyond the dreams of Roosevelt and Johnson combined. But in the government's war on poverty, poverty is winning and the casualties are the poor. Hope and opportunity are missing in action. Programs and policies that once were judged by the height of their aspirations must now be judged by the depth of their failure. This is no longer a source of serious debate, no longer a matter of partisan politics; it is a matter of national concern — a concern reflected recently on the covers of *US News* and *Newsweek*.

I have a belief that is confirmed by the record of our times. It is this: the greatest, most insistent human need is not subsistence, not hand-outs, not dependence, but independence. Not the kind of independence that suggests people don't need one another or that suggests that every man is an island. Quite the opposite, the independence of which I speak is the independence born of economic self-sufficiency and opportunity. The independence to dream, pursue, and fulfill our deepest wishes and our personal potential. This is something that the social architects cannot plan or build. It is not structure, it is spirit. It is something that our welfare system has lacked for at least the past 30 years. It is a reality that we continue to ignore only at our peril.

I believe it is time again to create a welfare system that helps, not hurts those it seeks to serve. That is the standard against which reform must be judged — not some utopian ideal, but the cold, hard realities of our present welfare system.

CIVIC ACT

Today I will introduce the Communities Involved in Caring

(CIVIC) Act. We have neither the aspiration nor the expectation that it alone is the long-awaited answer to our welfare problems. But we do believe that it is a significant step toward restoring the opportunities of dignity through independence and the access to the world of upward mobility.

This Act is predicated on three fundamental beliefs. First, that states need to be given maximum flexibility in reforming their welfare systems. Second, that our intermediary organizations — especially private and religious charitable organizations — need to be utilized in welfare reform. Third, that intermediary organizations need not only money, but volunteers, to flourish.

BLOCK GRANTS

The CIVIC Act block-grants Washington's four main welfare entitlement programs — AFDC, Food Stamps, Supplemental Security Income, and Medicaid — to the states. It does this first by capping the spending on AFDC, Food Stamps, and SSI at either an average of FY 1992-1994 levels, or at FY 1994 levels, whichever is higher. This cap would then apply for the next five years. For Medicaid, which is currently growing at rates exceeding 10 percent per year, spending would be capped at a rolling 5 percent increase for the next five years. These programs would then be extricated from their existing bureaucracies — HHS, Agriculture, etc. — and given to the Department of Treasury to distribute to the states.

Treasury's oversight role would be minimal because the only qualifications on the block grants would be the following. First, states would be required to make welfare recipients work. How best to do that. The nature of the work. The level of participation. All of those issues would be left to the states to determine. Second, states which decrease illegitimacy, using existing governmental statistics, will be able to use a portion of their block grant for elementary and secondary education or any other function they desire.

CONCLUSION

When he traveled through America more than 100 years ago, the great French observer Alexis deTocqueville was struck by how caring Americans were for each other. "The Americans' regard for themselves," he wrote, "constantly prompts them to assist one another and inclines them willingly to sacrifice a portion of their time and property to the welfare of [others]." What this Act seeks to undo is 30 years of Washington discouraging that very basic American instinct to help one another. These ideas are not new ideas. They are, in fact, ideas that have been tried, tested, and found successful.

READING

11

GOVERNMENT WELFARE CORRUPTS THE RICH

Peter Montague

Peter Montague wrote the following piece for Rachel's Environment and Health Weekly, *Environmental Research Foundation, P.O. Box 5036, Annapolis, MD 21402, 410-263-1584 (Fax), 410-263-8944 (Phone).*

■ POINTS TO CONSIDER

1. How did supply-side economics of the 1980s affect poverty?

2. What has happened to Americans' faith in the American Dream?

3. Discuss how corporations benefit from public assistance.

4. How should "assistance" for wealthy Americans affect the debate concerning assistance for low-income Americans?

Peter Montague, "Polluted Politics and Corporate Welfare," **Earth Island Journal,** Spring 1995: 28-9. Reprinted with permission of **Rachel's Environment and Health Weekly,** Environmental Research Foundation.

Clearly, federal "welfare" programs favor corporations more than people.

The Republicans argue that unleashing "free-market" forces — and reducing taxes for corporations and the rich — will allow the economy to grow so everyone can benefit. Unfortunately, when this "trickle-down" or "supply-side" theory was applied in the 1980s, (combined with a massive increase in military spending, up $174 million yearly from 1979 to 1992) it increased the national debt, made the rich richer, swelled the poverty rolls, and reduced the income and security of the middle class.

LOSING THE AMERICAN DREAM

The economy has been growing in recent years, but so has economic inequality. The U.S. Census Bureau reported in October 1994 that average per-capita income rose in 1993, but 72 percent of the growth went to the wealthy. A full 40 percent of the growth went to the top five percent, the group that Labor Secretary Robert Reich calls "the overclass." The top 20 percent of U.S. households took 48.2 percent of the nation's income in 1993; the bottom 20 percent received just 3.6 percent — an historic record for inequitable distribution.

From 1989 to 1993, the typical American household lost $2344 in annual income, a loss of 7 percent. Between 1970 and 1993, working people without a college degree — 75 percent of the American workforce — saw their wages decline 12 percent. Labor Secretary Reich said one important reason for the decline of wages is that growth in corporate profits is not being passed along to workers. The Secretary issued a stern warning: "If American business continues to pursue short-term profits at the price of insecurity and falling living standards for a large portion of our society, it will sooner or later reap the bitter harvest of popular rage."

In a recent national poll, 55 percent of American adults said they no longer believe that you could build a better life for yourself and your family by working hard and playing by the rules. Of those without college degrees, 68 percent said they no longer believe it.

CORPORATE WELFARE

Reich has said that since the mid-1970s, members of the middle class have turned into the "anxious class," afraid of losing their jobs and their health insurance, fearful for their children's future. The underclass has been steadily growing, permanently mired in the inner-cities, cut off from good jobs and hope. In 1993, in the midst of economic recovery and an expanding economy, an additional one million Americans fell into poverty (earning less than $14,335 for a family of four in 1992 dollars). Meanwhile, the overclass was scooping up most of the available benefits; the wealthiest two percent of Americans saw their incomes rise by 75 percent during the 1980s.

If our economy is to grow, Reich argues, we must prepare our businesses and workforce to compete effectively in global markets and this requires an end to what Reich calls "corporate welfare." Most of these subsidies and protections stem not from economic logic, but from political influence. From farm supports and tax breaks for oil and gas firms, to textile quotas and telecommunications regulation, these special industry entitlements force taxpayers, consumers and businesses to transfer resources to the corporate sector. These subsidies are also profoundly regressive because the ultimate beneficiaries of these spending and tax handouts are the shareholders of the subsidized industries, who tend to be wealthy already.

The Democratic Party's Progressive Policy Institute (which the *Washington Post* described as "moderate to conservative") argues that decades of free handouts from Uncle Sam to wealthy corporations should end because the money would be more productive if it were invested in retraining the workforce. Free handouts to corporations shield them from competition in the global market, ultimately weakening them. Unlike the vast majority of individuals who receive public assistance, most corporate welfare recipients are not particularly needy. A few examples:

• The Federal Bureau of Land Management (BLM) rents out public lands to ranchers for livestock grazing. In 1992, the BLM's annual grazing fee was $1.92 per animal, according to the National Wildlife Federation. But private landowners charge their grazing customers, on average, $9.26 per animal. The low grazing fees amount to a food stamp program for livestock grazing. In 1992, the government's below-market grazing rates cost the taxpayers an estimated $55 million in revenues.

• Another federal handout to corporations is the Department of Agriculture's Market Promotion Program. This year the program will give American companies $100 million to advertise

"Sam.....I trust you're keeping up with the payments."

their goods and services abroad. The corporations with out-
stretched palms include Sunkist Growers, Inc., (which received
$17.8 million in 1991-92 to promote citrus products), the
American Soybean Association (which got $10.4 million in
1992) and McDonald's (which was handed $456,000 in 1991
to promote Chicken McNuggets). Millions more went to Gallo
Wines and M&M/Mars.

- The U.S. government also subsidized mining on public lands by
  charging below-market rates for mineral extraction. Perhaps the
  biggest beneficiary of Washington's giveaway of mineral rights
  is the American Barrick Resources Corp., based in Toronto.
  Since 1987, the company has extracted $8.75 billion (yes, bil-
  lion) worth of gold from a site in northern Nevada that is the
  property of the American people. The federal government is
  now preparing to sell the land to American Barrick for all of
  $15,000.

- Major pharmaceutical companies are also subsidized by the
  government. While the government pays for a substantial portion of the research necessary to develop new drugs to fight disease, private drug makers are provided exclusive rights to market and profit from them. U.S. taxpayers spent $32 million over
  15 years to develop Taxol, an anti-cancer drug. Bristol-Myers

Squibb was provided extensive government data and exclusive commercial rights to Taxol in 1991, at which time it began charging patients $986 for a three-week supply.

- Some forestry companies signed contracts to purchase federal timber at a set price in the mid-1980s and then defaulted. These deadbeat companies now owe the U.S. Treasury $135.6 million. The scofflaws claim that they were justified in breaching the contracts because of falling lumber prices.

CORPORATIONS OVER PEOPLE

Last year, taxpayers spent $51 billion in direct subsidies to corporations and lost another $53.3 billion in corporate tax breaks, according to the Office of Management and Budget and Congress's Joint Committee on Taxation.

This $104.3 billion give-away to businesses contrasts with the $75.1 billion total cost of all federal welfare programs for individuals, including help for the blind and deaf, drug and alcohol treatment, assistance to the handicapped and elderly, care for the mentally retarded, children's vaccination and immunization programs, and food stamps (50 percent of which go to children). Clearly, federal "welfare" programs favor corporations more than people.

Not all subsidies are bad. Federal subsidies also support childhood immunization, middle-class home ownership, and health, safety and environmental regulation. These are government pro-

CORPORATE SOCIALISM:
AID TO DEPENDENT CORPORATIONS

Lo, the poor taxpayer! At all levels of government, thousands of companies are feeding at the taxpayers' trough. Washington has become a burgeoning accounts receivable for large corporations on welfare. So numerous and diverse are these programs, bailouts, subsidies, giveaways, loan guarantees, tax expenditures, tax breaks, inflated contracts, product promotion, protections from competition, grants and debt forgiveness that an umbrella phrase is needed to embrace them. "Aid to dependent corporations" reaches almost every sector of industry and commerce. It makes a mockery both of the customary Chamber of Commerce paeans to sink-or-swim capitalism and the prevailing ideology that ours is a capitalistic economy. Increasingly, corporate socialism is the economy for most of the GNP, excepting many small businesses that are still free to go bankrupt instead of going to Washington.

Ralph Nader, "Corporate Welfare," **Multi-National Monitor**, January/February, 1993: 42.

grams intended to promote social goals that benefit everyone, not just a wealthy overclass, and are needed to compensate for market failures. However, it seems doubtful that either the Republicans or the Democrats will be willing to cut corporate welfare.

The chief adversaries of social reform are these corporations, which have poisoned much of our land and water, harmed our health, polluted our politics, hijacked our democracy and diminished our common heritage. Until we get corporations out of our elections entirely, we probably will not be able to end corporate welfare.

Corporate America has diminished the American dream. The anger and frustration of the public are being manipulated by Newt Gingrich. For now, many of the targets of rage are immigrants, welfare mothers, government officials and gays. The challenge of reform is an unprecedented opportunity for organizers and activists.

Dan Cantor, executive director of the New Party, which was formed in 1992 as an alternative to the two major parties and is now active in 10 states, summed it up: "This election marked the end of liberalism, but not in the simplistic way Mr. Gingrich believes. The State has failed and the free market is failing. For most Americans, getting government off our backs is just one piece of the job. The real task is to get government on our side and to rein in a market system gone berserk."

EUROPEAN WELFARE STATES: CRISIS IN THE MAKING

Nicholas Elliot

Nicholas Elliot is a financial journalist in London.

■ POINTS TO CONSIDER

1. How has the economy affected many European social welfare states, particularly Sweden?

2. What is the largest social welfare expenditure in Europe? What problems does this pose?

3. Describe the type of reforms Europe is making to deal with their welfare crisis.

Nicholas Elliot, "A Crisis in the Making: Europe's Welfare Burden," **The Freeman**, September, 1994: 505-6. Reprinted by permission.

There is a crisis in the making across Europe, to which most governments are now alert.

Europe's welfare states face a profound crisis because aging populations mean growing numbers of benefit recipients and dwindling numbers of taxpayers to fund the entitlements. Prolonged recession has highlighted these dangers as high unemployment has meant higher welfare payouts and reduced tax revenues. As a result, wide budget deficits have developed in most countries of Europe, and there has been a sharp build-up of debt.[1]

This has awakened the governments of some European nations to the fact that maintaining "cradle-to-grave" welfare states is impossible in the long term, and reforms are already being undertaken to limit eligibility to benefits. As privatization was partly a response to the inefficiency of industry in the 1970s, so welfare reform is being forced by inexorable demographic strains. In years ahead, economic growth rates in the countries of Europe are likely to depend heavily upon their differing welfare burdens.

Comprehensive welfare states have become standard across Western Europe since 1945, providing — variously — unemployment benefits, sick pay, disability benefits, maternity benefits, child care, health care, and pensions. In the early stages it appeared affordable to extend these benefits, paid for by young taxpaying populations.

However, there was always a fine line. Sweden illustrates the economic consequences of unrestrained welfarism. From 1960 to 1990, as an extensive welfare state was erected, government spending grew from 31 percent of Gross National Product to 60 percent. But the increase in taxes required to pay for this blunted incentives disastrously. For instance, because of higher taxes, real after-tax wages for Swedish industrial workers fell 0.6 percent from 1980 to 1987 despite a 72 percent increase in gross wages.[2]

As a result, Sweden has tumbled from being the third wealthiest in 1970 to 12th place among rich countries, reflecting an average growth of only 1.1 percent in the past 20 years. The government of Carl Bildt was elected in 1991 with a program of welfare reform to restore the economy.

PENSIONS AND AGING

The largest spending increases in welfare states have been on pensions, and without reform the future costs are potentially

explosive. Only about a quarter of the increase in pension spending among Organization for Economic Co-Operation and
Development (OECD) countries between 1960 and 1984 was due
to aging populations; the rest resulted from widened entitlements
and larger benefits.[3] Because such a major aging is now under-
way, this largess will have to be reversed.

Greater longevity means that by the middle of the next century
there will be 190 million over-65s in the OECD, up from 61 million in 1960. The disparity this will cause between earners and
pensioners is highlighted by the age-dependency ratio, which
shows the number of over-65s in proportion to 15-64 year-olds.
This is set to rise from 19 percent in 1990 to 28 percent by 2020
and 37 percent by 2040[4]...

The fiscal stress of this aging will be exacerbated by some pension schemes reaching maturity — paying out the maximum benefits — around the time that the number of pensioners peaks.
When pension funds are first established there are many contributors and few claimants, but as time goes on there are fewer payers
and more recipients. For example, Britain's State Earnings Related
Pension Scheme (SERPS) will mature in 2020.

Many government schemes are unfunded; they are simple trans-
fers from the young to the old. Whereas funded schemes can be
managed with a view to future liabilities, unfunded schemes are
laid bare to the ravages of demographic swings. Also, older people make greater demands on health care, which adds to government spending where the system is publicly operated. For example, the over-75s cost Britain's National Health Service nine times
as much each year as 16-64 year-olds.[5]

THE NECESSITY OF REFORM

There is a crisis in the making across Europe, to which most
governments are now alert. The extent of their reforms now —
consisting principally of reducing government entitlements and
encouraging private provision — will be a key determinant of economic growth in years to come.

Several countries have raised the age at which government pensions are paid. The British government recently announced that
the pensionable age for women, currently 60 years, will be raised
to 65, equal to that of men. The Italian government plans to raise
the pensionable age from 60 years to 65. Bildt's government in

Sweden intends to raise it from the current 60 years to 61. In France the government plans to lengthen the period over which contributions must be made to qualify for a full pension. Outside Europe, Japan's pension age for women will be raised in the year 2000 from the present 60 years to 65, equal to that of men. The U.S. government took a similar step in 1983, scheduling a gradual increase in the pension age, from 65 to 67 years, beginning in the year 2003.

Another move has been to encourage opting out of government pensions into private plans. The British government did this with SERPS in 1988, prompting 4.5 million to exit the government scheme. This shrinkage in membership of the government scheme should greatly curb any increased costs to the taxpayer arising from its maturing.

The most significant reform is to update pensions with prices rather than incomes, as earnings typically outpace prices over time. The U.K. did this in 1980, and France did so in 1984. A British government actuarial report estimates that tax rates would have to be eight percentage points higher by 2030 if pensions had continued to be linked to earnings rather than prices.[6]

Differences in welfare burdens and in the rigor of reforms among the countries of Europe are already being reflected in their respective economies. Despite the demographic trends described above, Britain is in a relatively good position; her reforms will contain future costs. Also because much of the aging of her population has already occurred, the size of the emergent mismatch won't be as great as in other countries. The age dependency ratio is set to rise by 31 percent in Britain by 2040, as compared with 66 percent in the United States and 73 percent in Germany.[7]

By contrast, Germany's welfare costs are potentially explosive, with the admittance of new claimants from the former East Germany, placing further strains on a system that was already bloated. German government pensions are linked to earnings and the retirement age — 58 years — is relatively low. Proposals to reform a sprawling system of welfare benefits are already meeting with vociferous protest: 100,000 building workers recently converged on Bonn to object to plans to curb payments for being left idle by bad weather. The government may raise the pensionable age, but at the same time it is planning to extend government nursing care.

MORAL HAZARD

The fundamental problem of the welfare state will come as no surprise to its critics over the years: When it gives too much to those who are idle and takes away too much from those who are not, it destroys the incentives of both to work and produce. Theologian Michael Novak describes this as the "moral hazard" of the welfare state, its tendency to generate sloth and even dishonesty as seekers of benefits begin to cheat the rules and the most heavily burdened taxpayers begin to cheat the tax collector.

George Melloan, "Europe's Gloomier View of the Welfare State, **Wall Street Journal**, 14 February, 1994: A15.

Welfare costs are recouped in Germany through taxes on employers and employee earnings, not through general taxation as in Britain. As a result of higher welfare spending, these costs are expected to reach 40.2 percent of wages next year, up from 26.5 percent in 1970.[8] With such a burden it's not surprising that 36 percent of western German industries are planning to relocate investment abroad in the next three years.[9]

In the short term a welfare state may be an affordable luxury for a wealthy and prospering country, but in some European countries wealth and growth have been dissipated by the taxation needed to pay for it. Maintaining a welfare state is not simply a question of producing the wealth and then redistributing it, because the process of redistribution itself hinders wealth creation. The extent to which this point is understood will determine whether or not Europe remains a rich continent. It's an open question whether welfare reform will be far-reaching enough to restore economic incentives. Otherwise some European countries risk becoming economic backwaters.

[1] See S. G. Warburg Securities, **Weekly International Bond Market Review**, November 25, 1993.

[2] Peter Stein, "Sweden: From Capitalist Success to Welfare-State Sclerosis," **Policy Analysis**, Cato Institute, September 10, 1991.

[3] Organization of Co-Operation and Development, "Reforming Public Pensions," OECD, Paris, 1988.

[4] **Financial Times**, October 25, 1993.

[5] Paul Johnson and Jane Falkingham, **Aging and Economic Welfare** (London: Sage Publications Ltd., 1992), p. 133.

[6] Cited in Johnson and Falkingham, op. cit., p. 142.

[7] **The Sunday Telegraph**, November 28, 1993.

[8] **Financial Times**, November 19,1993.

[9] Cited in Gerard Lyons, The Outlook for the European Economies and Financial Markets in 1994, **DKB International**, November 1993.

98

EUROPEAN WELFARE STATES: PRESERVING SOCIAL STABILITY

Geoffrey Baldwin

Geoffrey Baldwin is a freelance writer in London.

■ POINTS TO CONSIDER

1. In what sense has capitalism failed Europe?

2. What has been the response to rollbacks of social spending in many European countries?

3. Assess the reasons for high job-growth in the public sector.

4. Discuss some of the lessons the United States can learn from the experience of the European Community.

Geoffrey Baldwin, "Farewell To Europe's Welfare State," **Toward Freedom**, October, 1993: 4-5. Reprinted with permission.

Most Europeans are determined to protect their hard-won social protections.

While capitalism has indisputably triumphed in the political realm, it is faltering badly as an economic system. In western Europe, for example, where unemployment rates seldom exceeded 3 percent in the 1960s and '70s, more than one in 10 workers are now jobless. And the long-anticipated cyclical recovery is still nowhere in sight.

The same politicians who presided over this disastrous slide are now arguing that the European Community's economy can be re-invigorated only through major reductions in social benefits. Segments of the public seem willing to accept the theory that comparatively high labor costs in Europe are hampering the EC's competitiveness and causing jobs to be exported to lower-wage, no-benefits countries. Opposition to high rates of taxation contributes significantly to this attitude. In most countries, social welfare programs are financed through payroll taxes levied on both employees and employers, and many workers have come to be persuaded by Thatcherite arguments that they are sacrificing in order to subsidize lazy fellow citizens and to finance bloated bureaucracies.

POPULAR SUPPORT

But most Europeans are determined to protect their hard-won social protections, and a few are actively resisting plans to dismantle the welfare state. Spain, for example, was briefly rocked by a general strike organized to protest proposed cuts in unemployment compensation. The Socialist government was consequently forced to rescind parts of its scheme.

The major political forces that have built and consolidated the welfare state are now demoralized and disorganized in western Europe. Social democratic parties have seen parts of their base slip away in recent years. And no wonder — in countries where they have long held power, such as Spain and France, the social democrats have failed miserably in their efforts to stem unemployment. In countries with once-powerful social democratic opposition parties, such as Britain and France, crucial numbers of their former supporters now believe this ideology to be outmoded and ineffective.

It is true that labor-based parties seem bereft of new ideas. And even if they were able to offer a bold and convincing blueprint for economic renewal, social democrats in any given western European country would probably be prevented from implementing it due to the increasing political homogeneity resulting from tighter EC integration.

The Community's members have agreed to follow an anti-inflationary policy that discourages spending on job creation. And that commitment can now be fully enforced as a result of the standardization of western Europe's central banking policies. Any deviation from the norm will bring swift and sure corrective action.

VOTER UNCERTAINTY

Most voters, while plainly worried about persistently high unemployment and the growing threat to social services, are uncertain about how to respond. Young people in particular, who are usually the main source of social innovation, are now generally apathetic and quiescent. Rather than becoming actively involved in politics, they devote their time to worrying about a bleak economic future. Unemployment rates for individuals aged 16-24 offer ample cause for fear and despair. In France ,the jobless figure for this group stands at 23 percent; in Italy, it is 28 percent; and in Spain, more than one in every three young people is without work.

Unorthodox movements of both the left and right, such as the Greens and various neo-fascist groups, are thus gaining support in several countries at the expense, mainly, of traditional progressive and moderate parties. The spreading violence against immigrants from developing nations is another symptom of despair over the disappearance of economic and social security.

Amidst this confusion and fragmentation, conservatives are finding it possible to proceed — slowly and incrementally — on the basis of their theory that decent benefits are not consistent with economic vibrancy. They regularly point to the conditions prevailing in east Asia, the former Soviet bloc and even in the United States. Unless we bring our labor costs more in line with standards in those parts of the world, the conservatives tell voters, we will continue to see our jobs exported to places like Hong Kong, Bratislava and South Carolina.

This argument is often buttressed by citations of the average wage paid to German manufacturing workers. Their hourly compensation, the highest of its kind in Europe, amounts to nearly $27. Almost half that sum — $12.50 — takes the form of benefits such as paid sick leave and child care allowances. By comparison, the average manufacturing worker in the U.S. earns only $16 an hour, with benefits accounting for just $4.50 of that total.

DEFENDING THE SYSTEM

Only a relatively few politicians are brave enough and sensible enough to point out that it is the United States, not Germany, which departs most radically from the standards achieved in the advanced industrial world. While abuses and seemingly extravagant perks attract the attention of the right-wing European press, most citizens of EC countries realize they enjoy basic protections against the vagaries of capitalism rather than indefensibly magnanimous give-aways.

SOCIAL JUSTICE

During the Reagan and Bush administrations a doctrine of rigid market economics and de-regulation produced...de-industrialization and criminal profiteering, to the advantage of the country's foreign competitors and the disadvantage of American consumers and workers.

American wages fell, with skilled employment lost and poorly paid service work substituted. Pensions and health protection were lost in many "restructured" companies, with overall absolute job losses and a rise in absolute poverty and homelessness, unknown since the Great Depression...

All of this supposedly was to produce efficiency. In fact, the U.S. economy and industry have lost ground to their principal industrial competitors, none of whom practices this form of ideological laissez-faire, and all of whom afford their people high levels of social protection and public amenity...

The theorists who brought us such policies still insist, against this evidence, that any governmental interference in the functioning of markets, or any serious attempt at wealth redistribution, destroys a nation's economic competitiveness. They refuse to recognize that Germany, Japan and France, among other countries, successfully combine highly competitive industrial performances with social justice.

William Pfaff, "Industrial Strength and Social Justice Can Coexist," **Los Angeles Times Syndicate**, 1992.

This is not to suggest that the welfare state serves only those genuinely in need of social assistance. In the Netherlands, for instance, nearly 20 percent of the workforce is collecting some kind of disability pay, often for nebulous ailments. It is also true that welfare-state bureaucracies, like any other large bureaucracy, are padded, inefficient and alienating. The only significant job growth in western Europe in recent years has occurred in the public sector, causing many of these systems to swell to gigantic proportions. But that is not mainly the result of patronage and feather-bedding. Social welfare bureaucracies have grown in accordance with the increasing demand for their services, which stems from the unemployment crisis.

This is the central dilemma — rising joblessness necessitates a greater degree of social assistance, even as the means of financing expanded services shrinks due to loss of payroll tax revenues. Meanwhile, a majority of western Europeans are at least skeptical of the conservatives' claim that the welfare state has created the condition for its own demise. But with the social democratic parties either discredited or lacking in self-confidence, few political leaders are pointing to other causes for western Europe's job drain.

Capitalists have, for example, failed to invest sufficiently or quickly enough in aging manufacturing plants. Huge profits have been squandered on speculative ventures while the EC's industrial base crumbled. Many goods can indeed be produced cheaper and better in east Asia, but that's only partly because wage rates are so much lower there.

The EC's own integration can also be seen as contributing significantly to job losses. Employment has actually boomed in comparatively low-wage member states like Portugal and Greece, with some of that growth resulting from the transfer of factories and offices in northern Europe. Perhaps there is a lesson here for Americans considering the merits of free trade with Mexico.

Much depends, then, on who proves able to set the terms of debate in western Europe. If conservatives and business interests are able to argue without convincing rebuttal, there is little doubt that the welfare state will slowly whither away. But if the left finds its voice, Europeans may yet manage to hold what they have won.

RECOGNIZING AUTHOR'S POINT OF VIEW

This activity may be used as an individualized study guide for students in libraries and resource centers or as a discussion catalyst in small group and classroom discussions.

The capacity to recognize an author's point of view is an essential reading skill. Many readers do not make clear distinctions between descriptive articles that relate factual information and articles that express a point of view. Think about the readings in Chapter One. Are these readings essentially descriptive articles that relate factual information or articles that attempt to persuade through editorial commentary and analysis?

Guidelines

1. Read through the following source descriptions. Choose one of the source descriptions that best describes each reading in Chapter One.

Source Descriptions

a. **Essentially an article that relates factual information**

b. **Essentially an article that expresses editorial points of view**

c. **Both of the above**

d. **None of the above**

2. After careful consideration, pick out one source in Chapter One that you agree with the most.

3. Summarize the author's point of view in one sentence for each of the following readings:

Reading **Two** _____

_____

_____

Reading **Three** _____

_____

_____

Reading **Four** _____

_____

_____

Reading **Five**_____

_____

_____

Reading **Six**_____

_____

_____

Reading **Seven** _____

_____

_____

5. Make up one-sentence statements that would be an example of each of the following: **sex bias, race bias, ethnocentric bias, political bias** and **religious bias**.

CHAPTER 2

CHILDREN, TEEN PREGNANCY AND THE DISABLED

READING

14

THE WELFARE SYSTEM SUBSIDIZES ILLEGITIMACY

William J. Bennett

William J. Bennett is Co-Director of Empower America, a conservative public policy institute in Washington, D.C., that places a major focus on national economic policy.

■ **POINTS TO CONSIDER**

1. What has happened to the rate of out-of-wedlock births in the African-American community, and all communities since the Moynihan Report?

2. Discuss the "economics" of single-parent households. Contrast this with the "economics" of two-parent families.

3. Summarize why society should be concerned with the rise in the out-of-wedlock birth rate.

4. What role has welfare played in "illegitimacy," according to Bennett? Do you agree with this? Explain.

Excerpted from the testimony of William J. Bennett before the Subcommittee on Human Resources of the House Ways and Means Committee, January 20, 1995.

Welfare is illegitimacy's economic life-support system.

I believe that any meaningful reform of our current welfare system must address the problem of illegitimacy. My statement will thus focus on the significance of the increase in illegitimacy; the attendant human cost; and the role of our current welfare system in sustaining and perpetuating illegitimacy.

THE INCREASE IN ILLEGITIMACY

This March marks the 30-year anniversary of "The Negro Family: The Case for National Action" — also known as the Moynihan Report, one of the most important pieces of social science ever produced.

This 78-page report, authored by Daniel Patrick Moynihan, now the senior senator from New York but then an assistant secretary at the Department of Labor, concluded that "[The break-up of the black family] is the single most important social fact of the United States today...At the heart of the deterioration of the fabric of Negro society is the deterioration of the Negro family. It is the fundamental source of weakness of the Negro community at the time...The family structure of lower class Negroes is highly unstable, and in many urban centers is approaching complete breakdown."

When the Moynihan Report was made public, *Newsweek* magazine referred to its "stunning numbers." The *New York Times* editorialized that "whatever the index of social pathology...it is apparent that the Negro family in the urban areas of this country is rapidly decaying." William Ryan of Harvard (one of Moynihan's most prominent critics) warned of "frightening statistics about broken Negro families, illegitimate Negro children, and Negro welfare recipients." Martin Luther King, Jr. categorized the existing breakdown of the Negro family as a "social catastrophe."

That was then. Consider now. In 1991, 68 percent of all black births were out-of-wedlock. Only 6 percent of black children born in 1980 will live with both parents through age 18, according to some projections. And more than 70 percent of black children will have been supported by AFDC payments at one point or another during childhood. In recent testimony at a Senate Finance Committee hearing chaired by Senator Moynihan, Professor Lee Rainwater predicted that by the end of the century out-of-wedlock birthrates for minorities will be 80 percent, while the out-of-wedlock birthrate for Americans as a whole will be 40 percent.

The Moynihan Report had little to say about the white family save that "the white family has achieved a high degree of stability and is maintaining that stability." Alas, that stability has now dissolved. During the intervening 30 years, white family structure has been severely eroded by high rates of illegitimacy, divorce, desertion and welfare dependence. White illegitimacy, for example, has increased from 4 percent in 1965 to 22 percent in 1991. The percentage of white females who are divorced has risen sharply. If these trends continue they will have even more serious consequences for American society than the decline of the black family, since whites constitute a much larger segment of the U.S. population.

This rapid, massive collapse of family structure is without precedent among civilized nations. Our country cannot sustain it; no country can. The American public in general — and the black community in particular — would surely give its collective eye teeth to wake up one morning and again face the "frightening statistics" of 1965. The Committee should consider this question: what words can adequately describe the situation we are now in? If "social catastrophe" described the situation three decades ago, what words can possibly describe our much worse situation now?

The Moynihan Report places our current social situation in historical context, and it clearly reveals two things: one is that the nation has taken a ruinous social tide over the last three decades. The other is that we have become in many ways inured to the trauma.

THE HUMAN COST

One thing we need to guard against is viewing these out-of-wedlock birth rates as sterile or abstract numbers. Behind these numbers there are real-life stories and tragedies and wasted lives. Although single women can do a fine job raising children — my mother was divorced and raised my brother Bob and me — it is a lot harder to do it alone. And we know that the chances of successfully raising children in a single-parent home are not nearly as good as raising children in a two-parent home. Every civilized society has understood the importance of keeping families together. They have known, too, that you cannot raise young boys to become responsible citizens unless there are other good men in

110

REDUCING "ILLEGITIMACY"

The problem facing America's low-income communities is not that too many women in those communities are on welfare, but that too many children in those communities are being born to single women and absent fathers. Reducing illegitimacy is not one of many desirable things to do. It is the prerequisite for rebuilding civic life in low-income black America, and for preventing a slide into social chaos in low-income white America...But the dominant reality that should be shaping the welfare debate is that the nation's low-income communities, black and white alike, are increasingly peopled by the grown-up children of unmarried young women and men who were utterly unequipped to be parents...As families have broken down, so have the neighborhood institutions for which families are the building blocks.

Excerpted from the testimony of Charles Murray before the Senate Finance Committee, April 27, 1995.

their lives — men who will spend time with them, discipline them and love them.

There is a large economic dimension to illegitimacy. Children in single-parent families are six times as likely to be poor as those in intact families; and far more likely to stay poor. Consider just two Census Bureau facts: (1) the family income of black two-parent families is almost three times the family income of white single-parent families; and (2) children in white single families are two-and-a-half times more likely to be living in poverty than the children in black two-parent families. The 1991 median family income for two-parent families was $40,137. For divorced mothers, it was $16,156. And for never-married mothers, $8,758.

But there is more — much more — than economics involved. Children in single-parent families are more likely to drop out of school; do poorly while they are in school; have emotional problems; become criminals; use drugs; be victims of violent crime; and be physically and sexually abused. In short, we are producing a lot of "at risk" kids. And as John J. Dilulio, Jr., professor of politics and public affairs at Princeton University, recently wrote, "they become juvenile and adult violent crime victims and criminal predators. They end up jobless and on welfare. They do drugs and get sick. A high fraction of the black males finish life in prison (nobody visits) and dead (nobody mourns) well before their time."

THE ROLE OF WELFARE

One of the reasons that I have some confidence in the direction the nation is heading on welfare is that increasingly there is agreement on two important premises. The first is the widespread acceptance of overwhelming empirical evidence: the current system is a complete failure. We have spent enormous sums — $5 trillion — over the past three decades on welfare programs, and what do we have to show for it? An underclass which is much larger, more violent, more poorly educated and which consists of many more single-parent families.

The second area of agreement is on an important moral principle: having children out-of-wedlock is wrong. Not simply economically unwise for the individuals involved, or a financial burden on society — but morally wrong. Even Secretary of Health and Human Services Donna Shalala, she of impeccable liberal credentials, said in an interview, "I don't like to put this in moral terms, but I do believe that having children out-of-wedlock is wrong." I hope that the Administration and the Congress enact legislation which is intellectually consistent with that analysis.

The relevant question, then, is the degree to which welfare programs have (unwittingly) promoted illegitimacy. I think a strong case — a commonsense case — can be made that it has contributed a lot. Welfare may not cause illegitimacy, but it does make it economically viable. It sustains it and subsidizes it. And what you subsidize you get more of. Welfare is illegitimacy's economic life-support system.

I believe that the intellectual debate about the role of welfare in fostering illegitimacy is essentially over. President Clinton helped end it when he said in an interview, "I once polled 100 children in an alternative school in Atlanta — many of whom had had babies out-of-wedlock — and I said, 'If we didn't give any AFDC to people after they had their first child, how many of you think it would reduce the number of out-of-wedlock births?' Over 80 percent of the kids raised their hands. There's no question that [ending welfare for single mothers] would work. The question is...is it morally right?" That is a good question — to which the answer is "yes." It is morally right because many more people would live better if we scrapped the current system, which subsidizes out-of-wedlock births.

I believe that making adoption easier is an essential and compassionate part of welfare reform. Adoption is the best alternative we have to protect a child's interest in a post-welfare world. The demand is virtually unlimited (at least for very young children), but current laws make adoption exceedingly difficult. Lifting restrictions on interracial adoption and easing age limitations for adoptive parents will help ensure that large numbers of children will be adopted into good, stable, loving homes. And for older children we must invest generously in the kinds of congregate care and group homes that provide order and love.

I will admit that there are no easy answers on this issue; every reform will involve some social dislocation. The fact is, no policy proposal is free of a potential downside. Unfortunately, we have inherited a disaster.

My own view is that ending welfare is prudent and humane — prudent because the social science evidence is in: illegitimacy is the surest road to poverty and social decay. And welfare subsidizes and sustains illegitimacy. It is humane because, again, many more people would live far better lives if we scrapped an entire system that subsidizes out-of-wedlock births. Here's "tough love" on a large scale: end welfare, and young girls considering having a baby out-of-wedlock would face more deterrents, greater social stigma and more economic stigma and more economic penalties arrayed against them if they have babies. There would, therefore, be far fewer births to unwed mothers, and far greater life opportunities for those girls.

I applaud the new Republican majority for taking serious steps toward dismantling the current welfare system. That you are willing to re-examine the core assumptions of current welfare policy is very good news indeed, as is the fact many Republicans are challenging the idea that AFDC, housing subsidies and food stamps should retain their status as open-ended entitlements. While I don't embrace every part of the welfare proposal outlined in the "Contract with America," I believe it is a good start. It is far better than what we have now.

WELFARE IS NOT RESPONSIBLE FOR OUT-OF-WEDLOCK BIRTHS

Rebecca M. Blank

Rebecca M. Blank is a Professor in the Department of Economics at Northwestern University in Evanston, Illinois.

■ POINTS TO CONSIDER

1. What is the author's view on the relationship between welfare and the rise in out-of-wedlock births? Discuss her supporting evidence.

2. How do out-of-wedlock birth rates in the U.S. compare to those of other industrialized nations? How do welfare benefits compare?

3. Evaluate the social factors that may contribute to the increase in out-of-wedlock births.

4. Discuss what has happened to welfare benefits in the U.S. over the past 25 years.

5. Discuss the potential policy options available to decrease teen pregnancy.

Excerpted from the testimony of Rebecca M. Blank before the Subcommittee on Human Resources of the House Ways and Means Committee, January 20, 1995.

*There is little evidence that the existence of cash-
assistance to low-income women has been anything
but a very minor factor behind the substantial
increases in out-of-wedlock births.*

The rising share of out-of-wedlock births is not primarily due to
the structure of existing welfare programs. There is very little evidence for the claim that welfare payments are driving the increase
in teen pregnancy. A wide variety of studies have related benefit
payments within the Aid to Families with Dependent Children
(AFDC) program, which is most typically referred to as welfare, to
fertility issues. Depending on which study one looks at, the
results either indicate that, once you control for other variables,
AFDC payments are not related to women's fertility or the effect is
relatively small. Robert Moffitt, a professor of economics at
Brown University, was recently asked to write a review of the
research in this area by the *Journal of Economic Literature*, published by the American Economic Association. After extensively
discussing all the studies, Moffitt concludes, "The failure to find
strong benefit effects is the most notable characteristic of this literature."

Since racial differences are often involved in the public discussion, it is worth noting that the research literature indicates that
the relationship between benefit levels and fertility behavior is
slightly stronger among low-income white women than among
African-American women. Among black women, there is almost
no persuasive evidence that benefit levels and non-marital births
are linked. There seems to be a weak positive link among white
women. Let me indicate other evidence that supports the conclusion that there is little relationship between welfare support levels
and rising problems of out-of-wedlock births.

THE EVIDENCE

First, as many have noted, the monthly support levels available
from AFDC and food stamps have fallen steadily since the late
1960s. In 1970, the typical woman with three children and no
other income would have received $900 (in $1992) from AFDC
and food stamps combined — the primary public support programs that help pay the monthly bills. By 1990, the typical
woman received around $700. It is hard to understand how the
recent rapid increase in unwed motherhood can be fueled by
public assistance payments when their levels have been declining.

115

Second, the rise in births among unwed mothers is not limited to those who rely on AFDC for support. It is a phenomenon spread throughout the income distribution. While higher income single women still have much lower rates of unwed births, their probability of giving birth has also risen substantially in the last 20 years. Non-marital births have also risen in virtually every industrialized country in the world. Unwed motherhood is a social phenomenon that is related to many changing factors, from increased economic independence by women, to decreased social stigma. To claim that it is primarily driven by welfare payments — available to only a small fraction of the U.S. population — is to miss the larger picture entirely.

Third, the cross-national comparisons here are very revealing. Relative to many other industrialized countries, government support for single mothers is much lower in the U.S. than elsewhere. Yet, the U.S. has one of the higher rates of single motherhood, and the highest rate of teen pregnancy. For instance, Canada is a country that is similar to the U.S. in many ways, both economic and social. In the mid 1980s, Canada's public assistance programs for poor single mothers provided about twice as much support as in the United States. Yet, Canada's illegitimacy rate continues to be below that of the United States.

I'm an economist and I believe in economic incentives. On the margin, I think the evidence indicates that variations in birth levels have a weak relationship to variations in AFDC benefit levels, with stronger effects for white women than for black women. But given the magnitude of the effects, there is no research evidence that would support a conclusion that the presence of AFDC has been in any way the driving force behind large increases in births among unmarried women. In fact, monthly payment levels have been steadily declining.

THE CAUSES

So what is the cause of rising out-of-wedlock births? Why then, has marriage among mothers declined? This is a big topic and, not surprisingly, there is a big research literature relating to it. The short answer is: There are many overlapping factors. Let me list a few.

1. Women's ability to find jobs and support themselves in the labor market has increased, increasing their economic independence. This has made marriage seem less attractive (it's not an

Yard showing batteries of privy vaults and dilapidated condition of steps leading to third story. Two room apartments rented for $12 per month. Pittsburg (October 28, 1908). Photo courtesy of the Social Welfare History Archives, University of Minnesota.

economic necessity for many women any more), and single parenthood seem economically viable.

2. Men's ability to support a family, particularly among men with fewer formal skills, has declined. Among both high school drop-outs and high school graduates, wage rates (adjusted for inflation) have declined substantially since the late 1970s, by 5 to 15 percent depending on the skill level. This is due to a host of reasons, as the demand for less-skilled workers in our current economy continues to decline. The net effect is that men are less attractive as marriage partners.

3. The social stigma associated with unwed motherhood has declined. For many young women, particularly in the African-American community, the acceptability of single parenthood has spread as more women become single mothers. This has occurred at the same time as sexual activity outside of marriage has also become much more common and widely acceptable in many parts of the population.

It is important to note that the growing economic independence of women and the decline in stigma associated with single parenthood has affected all women and explains a rise in single parenthood among women of all income groups, consistent with the evidence. The decline in the labor market opportunities among less-skilled men primarily affects less-skilled women, due to marital sorting, and explains higher levels of unwed motherhood among this group than among higher income groups.

In summary then, the primary causes of a decline in the propensity of women to marry are changes in the labor market and in the social acceptability of single parenthood that has influenced women at all income levels. There is little evidence that the existence of cash-assistance to low-income women has been anything but a very minor factor behind the substantial increases in out-of-wedlock births. In fact, a long-term decline in the level of this assistance over the past 25 years — years when the rise in out-of-wedlock birth has been steepest — indicates that welfare is not a primary cause of rising single motherhood.

WHAT OTHER POLICY OPTIONS DO WE HAVE?

Rather than adopting a scorched-earth policy, whereby all low-income never-married mothers are cut off from any form of a social safety net, there are other choices available to us. If we want to bring down the high rates of out-of-wedlock childbearing, we need to do the following:

1. Call upon the resources of American families and social institutions such as churches, youth organizations, schools, etc. to get the message out that it's not "ok" to be pregnant and single. In many ways, changing the social acceptability of single motherhood is something that the government can do much less well than other institutions, although the government can help fund demonstration projects run by other organizations that participate in this effort, and can provide a clearinghouse of information on effective programs. For instance, Title XX of the Public Health Service Act has funded a variety of evaluations on how to run effective programs that discourage teenage pregnancy.

2. Assure that our public schools function effectively, communicating the importance of education to their students, and a sense of the possibilities that high school and post-high school training can provide. Teenage girls who value a high school degree and post-high school training are much less likely to become pregnant

than girls who do not. Teenage boys need to receive the same message, so that the pool of men who are left out of an increasingly internationalized and skill-demanding economy shrinks over time.

3. For those women who do become single mothers and find themselves in economic need, make sure that public assistance provides not only cash assistance, but also a strong set of job training and job placement programs. The best thing we can do, within the context of our current laws, is to strengthen the Family Support Act, passed in 1988, to assure that teen AFDC applicants are immediately put into high school completion programs, with the child care assistance and health care assistance necessary to provide effectively for their children.

It is very tempting, and very human, to desire simple answers. Public policy would be easier to determine if welfare were the primary cause of rising single parenthood, and if eliminating welfare payments to never-married mothers would eliminate single parenthood without any other costs. Unfortunately, the world we live in is far from simple, and good policy requires that we reject such answers. Government programs are not the primary cause of these problems and changes in government programs will not solve them. Rising rates of out-of-wedlock childbearing are the result of multiple changes in the labor market, and in the social climate of this country. They will not be quickly turned around by any policy action of the federal government. That is an unfortunate fact of life, but it is one that we must face squarely.

If we want to decrease the incidence of single motherhood in this country, it will require a degree of social agreement and social will from all parts of society — from parents and grandparents, from civic leaders, from religious leaders, from those who teach school, and from all who serve as role models for young people. The message we need to send is clear: "Don't have children until you have the skills and economic stability to support them adequately. And when you have children, give them (and yourself) the advantage of growing up in a family with more than one adult who will live with them and guide them and love them."

Cutting public assistance to never-married mothers will merely increase poverty and all of its related problems among mothers and their children. Let's recognize the complexity of this problem and resist simple, easy — and wrong — answers that will only increase economic need among American families.

READING

16

FOSTER CARE AND WELFARE: REDUCING BIG GOVERNMENT

Conna Craig

Conna Craig is president of the Institute for Children, a private, non-profit group based in Cambridge, Massachusetts, dedicated to reshaping foster care and adoption.

■ POINTS TO CONSIDER

1. Summarize, in numerical terms, what has happened to the foster care system.

2. Analyze how adopted children compare to the national sample in the various social health categories.

3. What are the goals of the foster care system? Have state and federal agencies been true to these goals, according to Craig?

4. Evaluate how economic incentives can be used to place children in adoptive homes more quickly.

Conna Craig, "What I Need Is a Mom," **Policy Review**, Summer 1995: 41-9. Reprinted with permission of **Policy Review** and the Institute for Children.

Forty percent of all foster children leaving the system end up on welfare.

John, 10, is one of America's children who waits. He waits for a home, and he has been waiting nearly all of his life. When John was a toddler, his drug-addicted mom lost her parental rights, and claimed not to know who the father was. John has been legally free to be adopted since he was three, but instead has lived in state-run foster homes and group homes. While his childhood slips away, John's social workers debate his best interests and the programs they hope will address them. But this skinny kid who loves baseball knows better: "I'm all wrapped up in programs," he says. "What I need is a mom."

Across the country, there are 50,000 foster children like John, who no longer live with their mother or father and have been declared by courts as free to be adopted, but who languish for months or years in state-run, state-funded substitute care. On any given day, nearly 400,000 other children — none of them eligible for adoption — can be found in government foster homes, group homes, and shelters. Many of them are kept there by absentee parents clinging to the legal rights to their children.

Foster care and adoption in America have sunk to a state of near-catastrophe. According to the American Public Welfare Association, the population of children in substitute care is growing 33 times faster than the U.S. child population in general. During each of the past 10 years, more children have entered the system than exited. Every year, 15,000 children "graduate" from foster care by turning 18 with no permanent family; 40 percent of all foster children leaving the system end up on welfare, according to the American Civil Liberties Union.

What was for most of America's history an entirely private endeavor has become a massive, inefficient government system. State agencies consistently fail to recruit enough families for the children eligible for adoption every year; potential parents often are turned down because of racial considerations, or turned off by protracted and unnecessary waiting periods; cumbersome state regulations extend to private adoption agencies and can even prohibit private attorneys from handling adoptions. The result is that tens of thousands of children are now free to be adopted but have nowhere to go.

This is the dirty little secret of the welfare state: Every child is adoptable, and there are waiting lists of families ready to take in even the most emotionally troubled and physically handicapped children. Government adoption policies are utterly failing in their most basic purpose — to quickly place children who are free to be adopted into permanent homes.

The problem lies not with the children. What keeps kids like John bound to state care are the tentacles of a bureaucratic leviathan: a public funding scheme that rewards and extends poor-quality foster care; an anti-adoption bias that creates numerous legal and regulatory barriers; and a culture of victimization that places the whims of irresponsible parents above the well-being of their children.

I can identify with these kids. I was a foster child in a family that cared for 110 children. That family — my family — adopted me in the early 1970s. Years later, as a student at Harvard, I happened upon a book of statistics on children in state care. I was stunned to learn that decades of research, policymaking, and government funding had only intensified the system's failures. I was one of the lucky ones, but luck will not stem the tide of parentless children. By the year 2000, well over a million children will enter foster care, and tens of thousands of kids will become eligible for adoption. Unless the government apparatus of foster care and adoption is dismantled, these children could spend their childhoods wishing for what most people take for granted: stability, a family that will last longer than a few months, a last name.

SUBSIDIZING FAILURE

For years the rallying cry of many children's activists has been: "More money!" The National Commission on Family Foster Care, convened by the Child Welfare League of America, says that "family foster care and other child welfare services have never been given the resources necessary" to meet federal standards, and calls for a "fully funded array of child and family welfare services." When it comes to child welfare, rare is the research article that does not call for more money and further research.

America already is spending $10 billion a year on foster care and adoption services through public agencies. Federal dollars now account for nearly a third of all foster care funding, with most of the rest coming from state coffers. California alone spends at least $635 million a year on substitute care; the District of Columbia spent $53 million last year on a system that was so poorly run it recently was taken over by a federal court.

According to the ACLU, a year in foster care costs about $17,500 per child, including per-child payments to foster families and administrative costs of child welfare agencies. That does not include counseling and treatment programs for biological parents or foster parent recruitment and training. The *San Francisco Chronicle* reports that per-child costs for foster home or group home care have increased more than fourfold in the past decade.

The problem with foster care is not the level of government spending, it is the structure of that spending. The funding system gives child-welfare bureaucracies incentives to keep even free-to-be-adopted kids in state care. State social service agencies are neither rewarded for helping children find adoptive homes nor penalized for failing to do so in a reasonable amount of time. There is no financial incentive to recruit adoptive families. And as more children enter the system, so does the tax money to support them in substitute care.

By contrast, private adoption agencies are paid to find suitable families quickly, even if it means going out of state. The public social service bureaucracy, nearly overwhelmed by other urban problems, has little to gain by devoting extra resources to adoption. Private adoption agencies are free to focus on finding homes for kids and are financially motivated to do so. Private adoption agencies are paid according to the number of successful placements; public agencies, in a sense, are paid for the number of children they prevent from being adopted.

There is a similar reward for foster parents to keep kids in state care. By law, adoption subsidies cannot exceed foster care payments, and in practice they are almost always lower. According to the National Foster Parent Association, foster families in 1993 received anywhere from $200 to $530 a month for each child under age 10, plus additional money from states and counties. The subsidies are tax-free, and foster parents receive more money as the children under their care get older. So the longer the system fails to find permanent homes for kids, the more money flows to those fostering.

In some states, payments to foster parents caring for four kids equal the after-tax income of a $35,000-a-year job. The money is tax-free. It doesn't take much imagination to see that paying people to parent can lead to mischief. Parents are not held accountable for how they spend their federal and state allocations; for too many foster parents, the children in their homes are reduced to

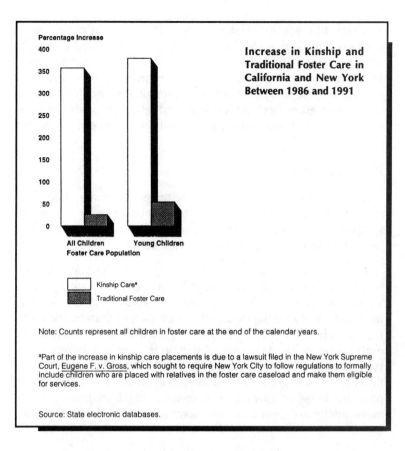

Increase in Kinship and Traditional Foster Care in California and New York Between 1986 and 1991

Percentage Increase

All Children
Young Children
Foster Care Population

Kinship Care[a]
Traditional Foster Care

Note: Counts represent all children in foster care at the end of the calendar years.

[a]Part of the increase in kinship care placements is due to a lawsuit filed in the New York Supreme Court, *Eugene F. v. Gross*, which sought to require New York City to follow regulations to formally include children who are placed with relatives in the foster care caseload and make them eligible for services.

Source: State electronic databases.

mere income streams. If foster parents don't wish to adopt the children under their care, what incentive do they have to alert other parents hoping to adopt?

Let me be very clear: There are many dedicated and compassionate people in the foster care system, serving as case workers, counselors, and foster parents. My own experience in foster care was a positive one. But I have seen and heard of too many that were heartbreaking failures...

THE FALLOUT

Attitudes against adoption, whether racially motivated or not, share at least two flaws. First, they ignore all the best evidence indicating that adoption leads to positive outcomes for kids. In 1994, The Search Institute of Minneapolis released the largest study ever of adopted adolescents and their families. The study, in which 881 adopted children and 1,262 adoptive parents were surveyed, found that children who were adopted fared as well as or better than a national sample of non-adopted adolescents in self-esteem, mental health, school achievement — even the amount of time spent each week helping others. Adopted adolescents were more likely to agree or strongly agree with the statement "There is a lot of love in my family" than were non-adopted children...

PAID TO PARENT

One of the reasons that foster care tends to ensnare children in a legal and emotional limbo is that its bureaucracy and incentive system attract parents who are unable or unwilling to adopt or help find homes for the children in their care.

Whether adopting through private or public adoption agencies, would-be parents must undergo a home study. Private agencies, which must successfully place children in homes to stay in business, are free to set higher standards for parents than public agencies do. Christian or other faith-based adoption agencies typically emphasize tough standards of behavior. But this is not so for state-run substitute care. In many states, adults who fail the adoption home study get a consolation prize: They can become foster parents. Deemed unworthy to serve as legal adoptive parents, these adults are then paid handsomely to raise children in state care.

Foster homes, group homes, and public orphanages share another vice: Their government money comes with regulations attached. This often guarantees confusion and conflict. Private orphanages always have been driven by a mission: keep girls from getting pregnant, keep children in school, expose children to the Christian faith, and so on. They use a combination of rules and rewards, discipline and love to fulfill their mission. Often, this isn't allowed in a state-run group home, where it may be against the law to hug a child, or to lock the door after midnight, or even to advertise for a married couple to serve as housemasters.

If a permanent, loving family is the surest route to producing happy, well-adjusted children, then what effect does the foster care system, at its worst, have on countless kids? The result of the system's delays, incentive structure, and regulatory grip is that many former foster children ultimately remain dependent on state services. They are wildly over-represented among welfare recipients, the homeless, and in juvenile and adult prison populations. In Los Angeles County, 39 percent of homeless youth are former foster children. In New York, 23 percent of the homeless were once in foster care; in Minneapolis, the figure is 38 percent. According to the Bureau of Justice Statistics, former foster children make up nearly 14 percent of America's prison population...

ADOPTION

I am convinced that there are more parents willing to adopt than there are children ready to be adopted. But the market for adoption is frustrated by the regulatory system now in place. To create a more efficient system, one with incentives to help rather than abandon innocent children, we must get Big Government out of the business of parenting. I do not mean we should create a market in babies. I am not talking about baby-selling. I am talking about serving babies and children by removing the barriers to their enjoyment of stable, loving homes.

Where parts of foster care and adoption are privately run, competition and incentives have led to better outcomes for children. In Michigan, where two-thirds of foster care management is privatized, private providers spend less per child, yet have achieved better social worker-to-child ratios than those of state-run agencies. Adoption is, in fact, the ultimate form of privatization: wresting authority over children's lives from the state and allowing children to be free, to be raised not by government but by parents...

Part of the problem is that government money extends indefinitely, with no sanctions enforced against bureaucratic delays. The Adoption Assistance and Child Welfare Act of 1980 required a "permanency plan" for every child within 18 months of entering foster care. This means that case workers decide whether to reunite a child with his family, place him in long-term fostering, an independent living arrangement, a group home, or make him free for adoption. Adoption is the permanency plan for 100,000 foster children, but no one knows how often these plans result in permanent homes for children.

When parents adopt, they can accomplish something government cannot: They can convince a child he or she matters. That's what makes adoption such a great gift, an expression of unconditional love and compassion. Don't we, as a society, owe that gift to our children?

FOSTER CARE AND WELFARE: EXPANDING FEDERAL RESPONSIBILITY

Marcia Robinson Lowry

Marcia Robinson Lowry is the director of the Children's Rights Project of the American Civil Liberties Union (ACLU).

■ POINTS TO CONSIDER

1. Discuss the author's concerns regarding block grants to states and the foster care system.

2. Summarize the effects of the Adoptive Assistance and Child Welfare Act of 1980.

3. How does the author account for the failings of the current foster care system?

4. Should the federal government modify its role in the foster care system, according to Lowry? Explain.

Excerpted from the testimony of Marcia Robinson Lowry, before the Subcommittee on Oversight Concerning Federal Child Welfare Programs of the House Ways and Means Committee, January 23, 1995.

In the absence of specific, enforceable federal standards, the half-million children in government custody have few rights against their state custodians.

Ever since the Adoption Assistance and Child Welfare Act (Public Law 96-272) became law in 1980, we have been bringing lawsuits against state and county child welfare systems for violating the minimal standards that are contained in that federal legislation. We represent tens of thousands of abused and neglected children in city and state child welfare systems and foster care programs around the country.

In 1980, Congress passed good legislation intended to protect children and to ensure that the billions of dollars spent in state child welfare systems was used as the opportunity to help and to protect these children, to intervene in their lives so they could have a decent childhood and the opportunity to grow up into healthy and productive adults.

The protections included in this legislation need to be strengthened and enforced, not eliminated. The federal government certainly needs to do a far better job in its oversight of the $3.5 billion dollars in federal funds expended in 1994 for foster care services. It cannot leave these programs unmonitored.

Even with the standards contained in Public Law 96-272, the states have not done a very good job. If Congress eliminates those standards, by providing child welfare funds to the states in a block grant, and if it eliminates federal oversight of federally-funded programs for abused, neglected and dependent children, these children are certain to be damaged even further. The consequences are truly unthinkable.

FEDERAL GOVERNMENT MUST SET STANDARDS

While we must allow the states to have flexibility in designing and administering their child welfare programs, and in deciding how to meet the standards contained in federal law, we simply cannot assume the states will provide adequate protection to children in the absence of enforceable federal standards and some form of federal monitoring and oversight. This is not an issue of trust; it is an issue of verifying whether the states are, indeed, using federal money to meet certain basic and generally accepted standards. We must remember that these children are more voiceless and powerless than any group in our country, and that if

Congress takes away the minimal protections provided by federal law, they will have none.

States are entitled to make their own choices about precisely how to care for their abused and neglected children, but the federal government must be a partner in this process if children are to be protected. Congress is both entitled and obligated to impose these minimal standards because it pays a large share of the costs. It is both necessary and appropriate for Congress to set basic standards on how this money should be spent, and on what general public policy goals it wishes to further.

The Adoption Assistance and Child Welfare Act of 1980 was passed by Congress in response to concerns about children drifting for years in state foster care systems. Though the statute imposes only minimal substantive obligations on states that choose to receive substantial federal funds to support their foster-care systems, it does require that states provide planning and services to children in an effort to shorten their stay in foster care and to protect children while they remain in foster care.

In passing the act in 1980, Congress noted that the federal funds provided under Title IV-A had not been used by the states to "move children out of foster care and into more permanent arrangements by reunifying them with their own families when this is feasible, or by placing them in adoptive homes," and that "there were significant weaknesses in program management which had adverse effects on the types of care and services provided to foster children."

Prior to the passage of this federal statute, children in foster care often had no chance at all to ever leave government custody. Adoption was something usually reserved for infants. If it did not take place within the first several months of a child's life, the child was considered unadoptable.

EXPLOSIVE NEED

State systems in need of widespread reform if they were to meet the minimal goals of the federal statute had barely had time to start developing their own approaches when circumstances changed. The number of reports of suspected abuse and neglect exploded , with a 130% increase from 1984 to present, an explosion related both to greater public awareness and better reporting procedures but also correlated closely with drug abuse, homelessness, and other serious social dislocations that have devastating

130

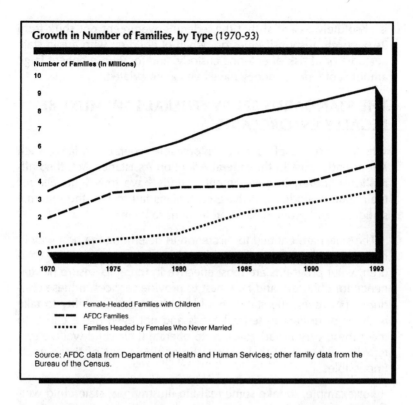

Growth in Number of Families, by Type (1970-93)

Number of Families (in Millions)

10
9
8
7
6
5
4
3
2
1
0

1970   1975   1980   1985   1990   1993

—— Female-Headed Families with Children
– – AFDC Families
•••••• Families Headed by Females Who Never Married

Source: AFDC data from Department of Health and Human Services; other family data from the Bureau of the Census.

consequences for children and their families. Second, children began entering foster care at a younger age, staying longer and manifesting increasingly serious problems — related in part to increased drug abuse by women — problems that make it that much more challenging to treat these children and find them permanent homes. Finally, there have been substantial reductions in state and local support for social service systems, reductions that have robbed child-welfare agencies of critically needed staff and service resources.

Given these forces, and the lack of federal effort to ensure implementation and enforcement, it should be no surprise that foster care systems are failing. However, it would be wrong to conclude that the federal Adoption Assistance Act has contributed to that failure. Rather, these systems are failing despite the statute's protections and despite the considerable federal resources that the statute provides.

The solution is not to eliminate the minimal protections we have. The solution is to make these protections more effective. It

131

is absolutely essential that the federal government not shirk from its oversight responsibilities on behalf of children who are in state custody, or at risk of entering custody, and for whose benefit large amounts of federal money have been appropriated.

THE STANDARDS SET BY FEDERAL LAW MUST BE LEGALLY ENFORCEABLE

In the absence of specific, enforceable federal standards, such as currently exist in the federal Adoption Assistance Act, the half-million children in government custody have few rights against their state custodians, if these custodians fail to met the minimal standards and provide basic protections to them.

The states are entitled to discretion to determine the best way to meet the federal standards and to provide proper care for children, what programs are most effective in trying to ensure permanence for children, and how best to provide services to these children. However, the states should not have the flexibility to take millions of dollars in federal funds and not even make efforts to meet these very broad goals, or to operate their child welfare system in such a way that makes the achievement of these goals impossible.

For example, to take some real-life illustrations, state child welfare systems in which the telephone lines set up to receive abuse reports often go unanswered are not making efforts to protect children. States which leave children in unlicensed and unsupervised foster homes are not experimenting with new program designs. States which determine that abandoned three-year-old children are adoptable — without trying to recruit adoptive parents for them — are not trying to find permanent homes for children. States which fail to provide any treatment at all for sexually abused children are not providing services to meet children's needs. Nevertheless, and regrettably, these situations exist in too many of our cities and states — all of which operate federally-funded child welfare systems.

The standards currently contained in federal law do not permit advocates to challenge a state for violating federal law based on the view that one approach to children's services may be better than another. It does permit advocates to seek protection for children, however, when a state does not even develop its own reasonable approach. Without such standards, and the right to enforce these standards, children are entirely without protection.

Increasingly, and in some measure because the federal government has not itself ensured meaningful implementation of the law, the standards in federal law have been used as the basis for lawsuits on behalf of abused and neglected children. For example: In the District of Columbia, caseloads were so high that one worker testified she couldn't develop plans for children — she just wanted to make sure that all the children on her caseload were still alive. Almost no children were adopted, because the District did such a poor job of recruiting adoptive parents and making children legally available for adoption.

Although the problems in the District of Columbia are well known, the problems in its child welfare system are not, unfortunately, unique to this city. Other systems have had similar problems, and lawsuits there have produced similar results. In Connecticut, a lawsuit was filed after the state social services commissioner likened the system to a "hospital emergency room" and decried the "senseless, merciless destruction and devastation of our children." The state agency was failing to investigate 60% of the children reported as abused or neglected. The medical needs of children in state custody often did not receive routine medical care, foster parents were so underpaid that committed foster parents had to reach into their own pockets to buy adequate food and clothing for children, limiting the number of people willing to provide homes.

It is an extraordinary fact that for many children in federally-funded state foster care, their time in government custody will be more damaging than the abuse or neglect they suffered originally. It is extraordinary that this is taking place at the expense of the federal taxpayers. For the most part, states have not complied with the existing minimal protections afforded to children in existing federal law. Nor is there any evidence at all to suggest that the existence of the law is in any way responsible for the deplorable state of child welfare services nationally. Eliminating rather than strengthening these protections will surely not provide any benefits to children. It will only leave them more vulnerable and unprotected than they already are.

GOVERNMENT PAYMENTS TO THE DISABLED: MAKING AMERICA ILL

Carolyn L. Weaver

Carolyn L. Weaver is a Resident Scholar and Director of Social Security and Pension Studies at the American Enterprise Institute, Washington, D.C. She is also a member of the Quadrennial Social Security Advisory Council and New Social Security Advisory Board.

■ POINTS TO CONSIDER

1. Evaluate what has constituted much of the growth of SSI in the past two decades.

2. For what reasons does Weaver favor "rethinking SSI for kids"?

3. Discuss the effect of Sullivan vs. Zelby (1990) on SSI.

4. What suggestions does the author make to reduce potential SSI fraud?

Excerpted from the testimony of Carolyn L. Weaver, before the Subcommittee on Human Resources of the House Ways and Means Committee, January 27, 1995.

For people with disabilities, SSI discourages work and, in providing cash support with basically "no strings attached," tends to perpetuate the very conditions that preclude work and promote dependency.

Under the pretense of "ending welfare as we know it," welfare reform would have proceeded without consideration of the single largest, and fastest growing, cash welfare program in the federal budget. Supplementary Security Income (SSI) would have remained on the shelf, where it has been for most of its 23-year history, largely immune to the scrutiny received by other federal welfare programs. The absence of serious scrutiny by Congress shows. The program is growing like gang-busters and serving a population that is very different from when it was created. It cries out for reform to address both specific problem areas, as well as more deep-seated problems in the underlying premises of the program.

PROGRAM GROWTH

SSI is more costly and growing much more rapidly than AFDC (Aid to Families with Dependent Children), the focus of the welfare reform debate. In 1993, the most recent year for which data are available, an estimated six million people received SSI, up nearly one-half since 1980 and one-quarter just since 1990. Federal spending stood at $23 billion, double its level (in real dollars) in 1980. Federal spending on AFDC, by contrast,was $16 billion in 1993, up 23 percent in real terms since 1980. According to the President's budget last year, the SSI benefit roll will grow so rapidly in the next few years that, by the end of the decade, the cost of the program (including federal and state spending) will exceed the cost of AFDC, food stamps, subsidized housing, the greatly expanded Earned Income Tax Credit, and all other major public assistance programs except Medicaid.

GROWTH AREAS — ALIENS

The great expansion in the number of aliens on SSI accompanied the huge influx of legal immigrants during the 1980s and early 1990s. Immigrants comprised 28.2% of the elderly on SSI in 1993, up from 5.9% as recently as 1982. The rapid growth in the number of aliens first moderated and then reversed the decline in the overall number of elderly SSI recipients. Indeed, were it not for the surge of aliens on the rolls, the number of elderly people on the rolls would have fallen quite significantly — by about 400,000 — since 1982.

DISABLED RECIPIENTS

Alongside the long-term decline in the number of elderly people on SSI, there has been an explosion in the number of disabled people on the rolls — doubling between 1974 and 1990, from 1.7 million to 3.4 million, and increasing by over one million in the past three years alone to about 5 million. Today three out of four SSI recipients are people with disabilities.

The typical person receiving SSI-disability is in his or her thirties, has a high school education or less, and, in contrast to the familiar image of someone in a wheelchair with a physical disability or someone who is blind, has been granted benefits on the basis of a mental disorder — schizophrenia, chronic depression, or anxiety, for example. While some of these conditions are obviously severe and generally disabling in the labor market, others are not and, in any event, are notoriously difficult to evaluate with precision. Fully one-third of adults on SSI-disability have a mental disorder — in addition to the one-fourth who have mental retardation. Young people with mental disorders are the fastest growing segment of the adult SSI population. The prospects that these people will ever return to work (or go to work) are very poor.

KIDS WITH DISABILITIES

Thanks to a 1990 court order and new regulations that loosened eligibility for children, together with other regulatory changes in 1990, children with disabilities are the fastest growing segment of the SSI population today. Stretching SSI in ways never contemplated in 1974, 225,000 children with disabilities (mainly mental disorders, including the much-discussed attention deficit disorder, and mental retardation) were added to the rolls in 1993, triple the number in 1989. The number of children on the rolls now approaches one million, or close to one out of five people on the SSI-disability rolls.

ADDICTS AND ALCOHOLICS

As highlighted by the popular press, even alcoholics and drug addicts have found their way onto SSI in growing numbers. According to the Social Security Administration, the number of people on the rolls with substance abuse as their primary disorder

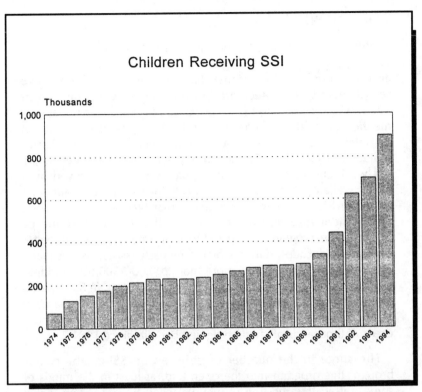

Children Receiving SSI

Thousands

Source: D. Koitz, G. Kollman, and J. Meisner, "Status of Disability Programs of the SSA, 1994," CRS Report for Cong. (June 6, 1994), p. 33, and Memo from M. Staren, SSA, to C. Weaver, Feb. 14, 1994.

(in other words, without some other qualifying disability, such as cancer or heart disease), nearly quadrupled in the 3 1/2 year period from October 1990 to April 1994, rising from 23,000 to 86,000. The legislation passed last fall took a step toward limiting payments to substance abusers.

RETHINKING SSI FOR KIDS

Between the rapid growth of the benefit rolls and news reports of kids being coached on how to behave "inappropriately" so as to qualify for SSI, the payment of SSI to children has become the focus of some controversy. There are two main concerns: first, are the kids seriously disabled within the meaning of the law, and second, are the payments needed? Poor families with kids on SSI receive much more support than other poor families.

TOP PRIORITY

With welfare reform a top priority, it is only appropriate to question the premises of this program — all the more because it was an afterthought in the original SSI legislation. In the massive social security and Medicare bill moving through Congress in 1972, which contained the proposal for SSI, there was not even a mention of children's benefits. Disability was defined in terms of complete inability to work and SSI payments were intended to replace lost income. The idea of payments for children (who did not work and had no earnings) apparently was conceived by a senior welfare official in the Nixon Administration, who, although the record is not clear on this point, managed to get a 26-word amendment inserted into the final bill without objection or debate. The program so created was of little note for the better part of two decades, during which time cash assistance was made available to a group of no more than 200,000-300,000 children annually. All of this changed in 1990. In that year, in Sullivan vs. Zebley, the Supreme Court ordered SSI to relax the criteria used for assessing disability in children and to review the cases of hundreds of thousands of children denied benefits since 1981.

The surge in the number of children on SSI-disability has brought this program into the open and, at least in the minds of some, raised the question of why we even have it, given that it appears to duplicate the purpose of AFDC, which is to help meet basic living expenses (such as food, clothing, and housing), albeit at a much higher benefit level, and Medicaid is available in either event. Proponents argue that the reason for the program is that disabled children are much more expensive to raise than other children. Surely this is true, on average. But it begs two questions — how much more expensive and how much of the expense is actually borne by the families?

Within the context of the current system, a good case can be made for converting the SSI payment for children — an unrestricted cash transfer that is unrelated to their special needs and may or may not be used to meet them — into a voucher that can be used only on the added costs of raising a child with a disability that are not met by other programs. Alternatively, expenses that are necessary but uncovered might be provided under the Medicaid program at federal expense. Either way, the idea would be to eliminate payments to families with no claim to them other than the presence of a disabled child while meeting the legitimate needs of families with extraordinary expenses associated with their dis-

138

abled child. Neither change would preclude more major reforms of SSI, such as providing block grants to the states in lieu of some or all of the current program. Addressing this aspect of SSI is important in its own right, but even more so in the context of welfare reform more generally. An unreformed SSI program could well become an escape hatch — albeit an expensive and poorly targeted one — for families who lose eligibility under AFDC.

BROADER ISSUES

Most importantly, for people with disabilities, SSI discourages work and, in providing cash support with basically "no strings attached," tends to perpetuate the very conditions that preclude work and promote dependency. In addition, there are problems of eligibility determination that dwarf those in other public assistance programs. Whether in assessing an adult's ability to engage in "substantial gainful activity" or a child's ability to engage in "age-appropriate activities of daily living," the government's decisions about who is disabled and to what extent are costly, complex, inherently subjective, and frequently disputed.

Considering the social security disability programs more broadly, serious questions remain as to whether these sprawling government programs — premised on the complete inability to work — are congruous with modern views of the potential and the abilities of people with disabilities. Despite dramatic improvements in science and medicine, in technology and information, and in the educational opportunities of young people with disabilities, which have improved the quality of life of people with disabilities as well as the job opportunities open to them, the number of people on the disability rolls has never been higher. In 1993, some 9.7 million people received checks from the Social Security Administration based on a disability totalling $56 billion. Most disability recipients are prime-age men and women; most will never leave the benefit rolls. The "once disabled always disabled" paradigm of social policy in the 1950s and 1960s remains deeply embedded in current government policy.

GOVERNMENT PAYMENTS TO THE DISABLED: KEEPING THE WEAK SECURE

James B. Gardner

James B. Gardner is a member of the national Legal Advocacy and Human Rights Committee of ARC, as well as past president of ARC. ARC, formerly the Association of Retarded Citizens, is the largest voluntary organization in the U.S. devoted to the welfare of the mentally retarded and their families. Total national membership is over 120,000 people, with approximately 1200 state and local chapters nationwide.

■ POINTS TO CONSIDER

1. Describe who receives the benefits of SSI according to Gardner.

2. What is the author's position on eliminating assistance in the form of cash benefits to SSI recipients? Explain.

3. Compare the cost of SSI yearly benefits with that of institutional care.

4. Does the evidence indicate widespread abuse of SSI?

Excerpted from the testimony of James B. Gardner, before the Subcommittee on Human Resources of the House Ways and Means Committee, January 27, 1995.

Many critics of the SSI children's program are ignoring the very real needs of children with mental retardation and other disabilities.

People with mental retardation who are SSI beneficiaries are dependent upon SSI (Supplemental Security Income) and Medicaid for many of their basic needs such as food, shelter, clothing, medical care and long term supports and services. About 825,000, children (302,000) and adults (523,000) under age 65 with mental retardation receive SSI benefits. Children with mental retardation constitute 44 percent of the total number of children who receive cash assistance through the SSI program and constitute a majority of the 66 percent of children with mental impairments receiving SSI.

PROPOSALS FOR REFORMING THE CHILDREN'S SSI PROGRAM

While there is no specific proposal before the Subcommittee at this time, ARC is extremely concerned about proposals which have come to the forefront of discussions. It is our understanding that a proposal may come forward to eliminate the federal cash benefit to children and, instead, to grant (or block grant) the money to the states to provide services, not cash, to the children whom the states choose to serve. We also understand that the proposal would potentially limit the definition of disability for children, specifically eliminating consideration of functional capacity when determining disability.

We believe that this proposal actually runs contrary to a key precept of this Congress: to reduce government involvement in the lives of its citizens. Rather, the proposal would disempower families/beneficiaries from making their own decisions regarding their own needs within the modest cash benefit amount and, instead, give the funds to the states to develop and provide new services within a specified menu. The proposal would actually reduce a family's flexibility in meeting the needs of the child with severe disability. It assumes that people with low incomes are incapable of making appropriate decisions regarding themselves and their children.

PROPOSALS IGNORE THE REAL NEEDS OF FAMILIES

Many critics of the SSI children's program are ignoring the very real needs of children with mental retardation and other disabilities and their families and are proposing sweeping changes to the program which will harm many families.

The maximum federal benefit for an individual in 1995 is $458 per month, less than $5,500 per year. By its very nature, the SSI program provides only a very minimal income subsidy which does not even bring people to the federal poverty line. Families with children with severe disabilities who labor to provide for their children and to plan for their future are struggling on the edges of economic survival. Any type of emergency or unexpected expense could throw many of these families into an economic tailspin. They depend upon the cash which they receive to maintain the family's existence.

Despite the recent sensational news stories regarding the children's SSI program, the vast majority of eligible children benefit from the cash assistance program because it allows their families to meet their needs for food, clothing, shelter, and other basic necessities or goods. Families are able to tailor expenditures based upon the child's current needs and the unique circumstances of the family and are more able to respond to changing or unusual circumstances than typical service systems approaches. In addition, substituting more services for cash will not address the children's and families' needs for income support to supply basic necessities such as food, clothing, and shelter. We believe that the current mix of SSI cash benefits and the services available through various educational, social services, and health/medical agencies is better suited to meeting the complex variety of a child's needs than an all-or-nothing approach: neither an all-cash approach nor an all-services approach will meet the wide variety of needs in a child's life. Both are required.

Many parents of SSI-eligible children with disabilities report that their families would fall apart if the cash benefits were to be discontinued. They point out that they are able to keep their children at home, with the family, rather than in an institution, because of the assistance of the SSI cash. Many are fearful of what will happen to them and their children if cash benefits are halted. Many will be homeless.

If not from a humanitarian view of family and the value of a loving family to a growing child, then from a purely fiscal point of view, the Subcommittee should listen to the pleas of these families. The average cost of institutionalization in this country for people with mental retardation is over $77,434 per year. The combination of the availability of special education services and SSI benefits for low-income families has significantly reduced the rate of institutionalization of children. In 1969, of the almost 200,000 people with mental retardation living in institutions, about 95,000 were children. Today, it is estimated that only 65,000 people with mental retardation are living in institutions and only 6,000 are under age 21. The significance of this social change should not be ignored; we should not help to reinstate the economic pressures which may ultimately force families to institutionalize their children with severe disabilities. The savings to government are significant, also: combining the average annual costs of special education ($10,000 per student) with the maximum federal SSI benefit (less than $5,500) results in annual costs of about $15,500 per child — a savings of $62,000 per year per child versus the costs of institutionalization.

STUDIES DO NOT BEAR OUT REPORTS OF WIDESPREAD ABUSE

Contrary to the conclusions drawn from sensational anecdotal stories in the media and elsewhere, data from three recent federal government studies and reports of the growth in the children's SSI program (General Accounting Office; Social Security Administration internal review; and Department of Health and Human Services Office of Inspector General [OIG]) indicate that there is not widespread abuse of the system or attempts by parents or children to "fake" disability. The GAO reports that 70 percent of the children who are found eligible for SSI are found eligible on the basis of the medical standards of severity in the "listings." Yet the proposed reforms to the program are designed to broadly sweep away all of the good aspects of the program as well as those areas where improvements could be made.

Congress must also recognize that the Social Security Administration will continue in its ability to thoroughly monitor the children's SSI program, and other programs within its responsibility, unless adequate resources are appropriated for administrative expenses. ARC is willing to work with Congress and the Administration to identify and develop appropriate remedies for the problems that actually exist in the children's SSI program. However, ARC will continue to oppose sweeping changes which are harmful to the vast majority of children and their families and which have no basis other than in sensational, anecdotal stories. We believe that a thorough discussion of the problems that exist in the children's SSI program requires an understanding of the history and development of the various components which make up the process for determining childhood disability.

CRITERIA

In 1990, Social Security Administration (SSA) appointed a panel of experts in child development and childhood disability to help the agency develop criteria for determining disability based on an individualized functional assessment. The experts represented a wide range of areas: general pediatrics, developmental genetics, developmental pediatrics, infant development, behavioral pediatrics, pediatric psychology, pediatric neurology, child psychology, pediatric special education, home and community care, family and support systems, physical and occupational deficits, early childhood education, pediatric rehabilitation, learning disorders, chronic illness and somatics, and communication disorders.

New regulations for determining childhood disability on the basis of functional limitations were published by SSA and were immediately effective on February 11, 1991 as interim final regulations. Final regulations were published on September 9, 1993 with a sunset date of Sept. 9, 1997, when SSA will further review the implementation of the regulations and consider any necessary changes.

MUCH NEEDED IMPROVEMENTS FOR CHILDREN

In a nutshell, the final rules for childhood disability determination, the childhood mental impairment regulations, and the regulations for Down syndrome and other serious hereditary, congenital, or acquired disorders were the result of much careful deliberation over the course of nearly a decade and involved numerous experts on child development and disability. While there are some problems as discussed above, overall the new regulations are a tremendous improvement for children and long overdue. After 20 years, children are just now beginning to receive the consideration of their disabilities which should have occurred from the beginning of the program. With such a long delay in implementation of the original intent of the program, it is no wonder that the numbers of children becoming eligible for the program are increasing rapidly. The dramatic increase in the numbers of eligible children must be seen in historical context and must not be allowed to serve as the basis for inappropriate cutbacks.

CONCLUSION

As discussed above, where there are problems, solutions must be carefully and surgically crafted to ensure that they are not overreaching in effect. Frankly, we believe that many of the "problems" which have been reported are the result of misunderstandings of the SSI program, generally, and of the process for determining childhood disability, specifically. Where instances of abuse or exploitation are suspected, proper avenues for redress exist in the state child protective services systems and within the SSA representative payee system.

EXAMINING COUNTERPOINTS:
Orphanages and Welfare

This activity may be used as an individualized study guide for students in libraries and resource centers or as a discussion catalyst in small group and classroom discussions.

The Point

The "Orphanage Fantasy" is conservative propaganda supporting attempts to blame America's poor for the profound national
problems of hunger, crime, inner-city chaos, low-wage jobs, and
the over forty million Americans below the poverty line. All this
occurs in a nation where rich people and corporations grow
wealthier, while having eliminated 400,000 well-paying jobs
since 1980. The orphanage idea is about depriving young,
unmarried, poor women of their children and more importantly,
forcing them into the labor force to further drive down wages for
millions of low-paying service jobs.

The Counterpoint

The orphanage is one humane alternative to the disastrous wel-
fare-foster care system. This system traps children in a state of
limbo and attempts to preserve families that are abusive and
hopeless while promoting a national bias against adoption. A
more humane child welfare policy would abandon the fantasy
that all families can be preserved and would insist on speedy termination of parental rights in cases of neglect and abuse.
Orphanages are especially worth considering for older children
who are hard to handle or suspicious of family settings.

Guidelines

Part 1
Examine the counterpoints above and then consider the following questions.

1. Do you agree more with the point or counterpoint? Why?

2. Which reading in Chapter Two best illustrates the point?

3. Which reading best illustrates the counterpoint?

Part B
Social issues are usually complex, but often problems become oversimplified in political debates and discussions. Usually a polarized version of social conflict does not adequately represent the diversity of views that surround social conflict. Examine the counterpoints above. Then write down other possible interpretations of the issue identified in the counterpoints.

CHAPTER 3

CHARITY, CHURCH AND WELFARE

READING

20

CHURCHES AND WELFARE: POINTS AND COUNTERPOINTS

Robert A. Sirico vs. David Beckmann

The following counterpoints examine the role of churches and welfare programs. The first statement is from Father Robert A. Sirico, President of the Acton Institute for the Study of Religion and Liberty in Grand Rapids, Michigan. The counterpoint is presented by David Beckmann, President of Bread for the World, a Christian citizens' movement against hunger with over 44,000 members.

■ POINTS TO CONSIDER

1. Explain the concept of subsidiarity.

2. How does Father Sirico feel private charities would fare in the absence of federal welfare programs?

3. How does Beckmann feel private charities would fare in the absence of federal welfare programs?

4. Discuss the effect of federal nutrition programs.

5. Do you feel that private charity should be exclusively responsible for the needs of the poor? Why or why not?

Excerpted from the statements of Father Robert A. Sirico and David Beckmann before the Subcommittee on Human Resources of the House Ways and Means Committee, January 20 and February 2, 1995.

While I hold the federal government partially responsible for the soaring illegitimacy rates since the beginning of the Great Society, I am not asking federal officials to solve the problem themselves. In my view the federal government should not now try to tinker with its welfare programs to punish women who give birth to children outside of marriage.

As I said, illegitimacy is a moral problem. And the federal government is not, and indeed, cannot be, an effective moral teacher. Church-State separation requires the welfare bureaucracy to remain morally neutral. And it cannot effectively promote sexual responsibility from a morally-neutral pulpit.

Subsidiarity

Rather than federal solutions, I believe there is a principle that should guide any and all efforts toward welfare reform: *subsidiarity*. The concept is this: those social functions that can be accomplished by a lower order of society should not be usurped by a higher order. When it comes to caring for women who are pregnant out-of-wedlock, the resources of first resort should be individuals, churches, neighborhoods, towns and cities. The federal government has tried to solve American family problems and it has failed. Now it must allow these mediating institutions to take over.

The idea of devolving social responsibility to the states is in keeping with the principle of subsidiarity. It is a step in the right direction. By itself, however, it is not enough. We do not want Washington bureaucracies to be replaced by equally intrusive government bureaucracies in state capitols.

When dealing with the illegitimacy problem, the very nature of the welfare state — with its bureaucratic, one-size-fits-all policies — precludes it from helping individuals become responsible parents and citizens. Indeed, it takes a much deeper understanding of human needs to encourage this.

Furthermore, the very existence of the welfare state lessens the incentive for individuals to become personally involved in problems like illegitimacy. This lessens their contact with and sensitivity to those in need. Under the current system, bad charity has driven out good charity. If and when bad charity comes to an end, we can expect an explosion of interest in helping those in need. We must begin to have faith in the good efforts of the American people.

Let me anticipate an objection. Some will say that what is called the "private sector" cannot take care of the problem — it is necessary but not sufficient. Let me submit that we have forgotten just how powerful the forces of genuine charity are in American society. For too long, the federal government has crowded out private solutions. Once severe budgetary changes begin to remind people of their responsibilities to others, we will be astonished at the outpouring of energy. Let's try to remember that government has no monopoly on compassion. Indeed, government is compassion's least able practitioner.

Let's allow real charities, not bureaucracies, to take on the illegitimacy problem. Along with the material assistance for mothers who are pregnant out-of-wedlock, charities can administer individual care that is catered to a woman's specific circumstances, needs, abilities, and character.

Will a cutoff of parental aid lead to an increase in abortion? No. Abortion is not a cost-free decision. It is the most difficult and painful decision a woman can make. Far from encouraging abortion, removing subsidies will discourage promiscuity. For a person of free will, it will clarify the issue of whether to risk pregnancy in the first place. We cannot, of course, guarantee perfect results, but we can stop subsidizing the current crisis.

Religious Values

The alternative to the current welfare system is to organize the care of at-risk young people in a manner that allows for the influence of religious values. The government need only allow this to happen; it need not promote it. By gradually eliminating federal benefits, which impose no concrete responsibilities on the part of the recipient, poor women who are pregnant out-of-wedlock will have to turn to more local organizations, which include church, synagogue or mosque-run charities.

Think of the change in incentives that would result. If another baby means no hardship and a bigger check, it is easy to see why this is not wholly undesirable from one point of view. Yet, if the individual's circumstance is being closely monitored by a secular charity or church ministry, the individual becomes acutely aware that sexual irresponsibility has a price.

151

The church very likely views sex outside of marriage as a sin, and will not provide services without admonition or some form of work in return. As an organic part of a church ministry, the individual becomes accountable to those who are providing the aid. The close contact with the providers discourages irresponsible behavior.

This model relies on the classical view of moral tutoring which is two-dimensional: we abstain from immoral behavior because we fear its effects and we abstain because we love the good. Church-run charities hope to instill a love of good in the people they help. Yet clients may also fear a reprimand or a loss of services. Fear and love are both motivators. While the latter is a preferable motive, the former is also effective.

Effective charities will thrive on their own. Yet, steps must be taken to allow them to flourish. We need to make charitable giving more financially rewarding. For example, we could allow individuals to deduct 110 percent of their charitable contributions, thereby increasing the incentive to give. Or tax deductions could be replaced with a tax credit, which would allow people to choose to use their money to support either public or private systems of welfare provision.

Whatever policy routes are taken, the ultimate goal should be to return responsibility to individuals, churches, neighborhoods, towns and cities. Every case of family tragedy is different, and the individuals involved have different resources, abilities, and weaknesses. A faceless bureaucracy cannot take all of these into account. Nor can it encourage moral renewal. What people need is not layers of public agencies, but other human beings who have knowledge of their real needs and a commitment to help them become responsible and independent citizens.

DAVID BECKMANN: THE COUNTERPOINT

My name is David Beckmann. I am the President of Bread for the World, a Christian citizens' movement against hunger. We have 44,000 members. Sixty denominations and 3,500 churches of many theological perspectives support Bread for the World. We [Bread for the World] would like to register our strong opposition to merging food assistance programs into a single block grant as part of welfare reform. Many things in our welfare system need changing, and we support reforms that would effectively help employable poor people move into jobs that would enable them to support their families. But it will take an extraordinary commitment on the part of government, the private sector and the individual to make this possible on a large scale.

The welfare debate should not be about cutting dollars but about becoming more effective in reducing hunger and poverty. Polls show that people don't want to cut food assistance and are especially open to spending more on poor children. We should spend more money now for prevention programs like WIC and Head Start; they save money in the long run. It also makes sense to pay for necessary remedial education, job training, job creation, low-wage subsidies, and assistance with child care and health care so that people can get into the workforce.

Federal Food Programs Are Effective

One of the things government has figured out how to do well over the past 30 years is to provide basic nutrition for those who are disadvantaged. This is a good investment, since adequate diets are essential for healthy development and productive work. Just after the Second World War, the country recognized — because many recruits were not eligible to serve due to the effects of malnutrition — that child nutrition is essential to national security. The School Lunch Program was started to remedy that problem. Gradually, our nation has put together a comprehensive nutrition safety net composed of federal food assistance programs for pregnant women, pre-school and school-age children, adults, and senior citizens. It would be short-sighted for the federal government to wash its hands of the responsibility to assure an adequate diet for all its citizens.

In the mid-1980s the bipartisan Committee on Federalism and the National Purpose chaired by Republican Senator Dan Evans investigated turning some federal programs over to the states. They concluded that the federal government should take on an even larger responsibility for seeing that poor children were assured basic benefits. "Whenever it occurs, poverty is a blight on our whole society," the Committee reported, "and Americans in similar circumstances should be treated alike. Children whose early years are damaged by the effects of poverty in one state may later become voters, employees, and possibly welfare recipients in other states."

The federal food programs work.

- WIC reduces infant mortality, low birthweight, and anemia. It improves cognitive skills. A panel of Fortune 500 CEOs testified before this body in 1991 that "WIC is the health-care equivalent of a triple-A rated investment."

- School lunch provides children with one-third or more of the Recommended Dietary Allowance for key nutrients.

- Food stamps increase the nutritional quality of diets by 20 to 40 percent.

- Elderly Nutrition Programs improve the nutritional health of older people, who are particularly vulnerable to malnutrition.

Churches Are Already Doing Their Part

Some members of Congress have said that churches can bear yet more of the costs for feeding and sheltering people in need. The Personal Responsibility Act, H.R. 4, cuts $60 billion from welfare and food programs over the next four years. If the 350,000 churches in America would have to make up for that cut, they would all need to add $170,000 to their budgets over the four years. This is completely unrealistic.

We've tried the thousand-points-of-lights to deal with hunger. Hunger increased in the early 1980s, partly because Congress cut social programs then. Churches and others across the country have responded to growing hunger with a private feeding movement. There were very few soup kitchens in 1980; now there are

150,000 private feeding agencies passing out food to hungry peo- ple in our country. Private charities have been diverted from encouraging personal responsibility — alcohol and drug rehabili- tation, for example — into just feeding people month by month.

And the explosive growth of the private feeding movement has failed to keep pace with the growth of hunger. Ask at any soup kitchen or food pantry in any low-income neighborhood. The federal government must do its part. Let me also make a theologi- cal point. The Bible teaches that God holds societies responsible for justice toward people in need. The prophets held kings — their government structure — primarily responsible. The Bible also urges individuals to be charitable, but charity is no substitute for justice.

We urge you to maintain the federal government's role in pro- viding a safety net for needy children, families, and elderly peo- ple. This can best be done by keeping national nutrition and eli- gibility standards, preserving entitlement status for food stamps, child nutrition and Aid to Families with Dependent Children, and increasing funding for WIC to reach all eligible low-income women, infants, and children.

155

READING

21

PRIVATE CHARITY VS. PUBLIC WELFARE: THE POINT

Peter J. Ferrara

Peter J. Ferrara is a Senior Fellow at the National Center for Policy Analysis. The Center is a politically conservative non-profit, public policy research institute founded in 1983 and internationally known for its studies on public policy issues. Located in Dallas, Texas, the center draws an international network of academic advisors.

■ **POINTS TO CONSIDER**

1. What does the author believe the key components of welfare reform to be?

2. Discuss the author's feelings about the role government plays in aiding those in need.

3. Why is the private sector better at delivering service to the needy, according to Ferrara?

4. Summarize the author's attitude toward "entitlement" status for welfare benefits.

Excerpted from the testimony of Peter J. Ferrara before the Subcommittee on Human Resources of the House Ways and Means Committee, January 30, 1995.

A mountain of evidence and experience indicates that private charities are far more effective than public welfare bureaucracies.

Simply stated, the current welfare system is a disaster for the poor, the taxpayers, the economy and the nation. Reform of the system should be based on two key components. First, all major federal welfare programs should be abolished and the money currently spent on these programs should be given to the states in the form of "block grants." Second, taxpayers should be allowed to shift that funding from state programs to private charities.

BLOCK GRANTS

Federal funding for as many current federal welfare programs as possible should be sent to the states with only one proviso: that the funds be used to help the poor. Each state would then be able to use the funds, along with the current state welfare funds, to design its own welfare programs. These grants would replace AFDC, food stamps and public housing, among other so-called entitlement programs. Medicaid funds could be segregated in a separate grant with the requirement that they be spent on health care for the poor. This would free each state to experiment with entirely new approaches to welfare. States might offer work instead of welfare. They might grant funds to well-run private charities. They might come up with entirely new approaches that no one has thought of yet.

THE PRIVATE CHARITY TAX CREDIT

The second component of reform would be a dollar-for-dollar tax credit for contributions to private charities. Taxpayers could donate up to 40 percent of their personal income tax payments, which is the share of total individual income taxes that currently goes to federal means-tested welfare programs. To the extent that a state's taxpayers utilized such credits, the state's welfare block grants would be reduced by an equal amount. Thus the revenue loss from the tax credits would be offset completely by reduced federal welfare grants to the states, leaving no effect on the deficit.

Block grants plus tax credits would give taxpayers the ultimate control over welfare. If a state misspent its block grant funds, its taxpayers could shift the funds to the private alternatives that work better. Healthy market competition between the state programs and private charities would give state welfare bureaucracies a real incentive to perform well in reducing poverty.

A mountain of evidence and experience indicates that private charities are far more effective than public welfare bureaucracies. Instead of encouraging counterproductive behavior, the best private charities use their aid to encourage self-improvement, self-sufficiency and ultimate independence. The assistance to private charities may be contingent on ending drug use and alcoholism, improving necessary education and work habits, avoiding out-of-wedlock births, maintaining families and other positive behaviors. Private charities are also much better at getting aid promptly to those who need it most and at getting the most benefit out of every dollar.

With the tax credit, private organizations would be able to compete on a level playing field for welfare tax dollars. To the extent they convinced the taxpayers that they were doing a better job than state bureaucracies, private charities, rather than government, would be permitted to manage America's war on poverty.

PUBLIC SECTOR FAILURES VS. PRIVATE SECTOR SUCCESSES

Although volumes have been written about the failures of government welfare programs, the academic and scholarly community has paid surprisingly little attention to private sector charity. Yet the private sector is playing an extremely important role:

- In 1992, total charitable contributions reached $124 billion, with contributions by individuals accounting for 82 percent ($101.83 billion) of that total.

- More than 85 percent of adult Americans make some charitable contribution each year.

- About half the adult population did volunteer work in 1991, contributing more than 20 billion hours of labor.

- The dollar value of these contributions of time is at least $176 billion.

- If the value of volunteer labor is included, private sector contributions to charitable causes are approximately the same as the poverty budgets of federal, state and local governments combined.

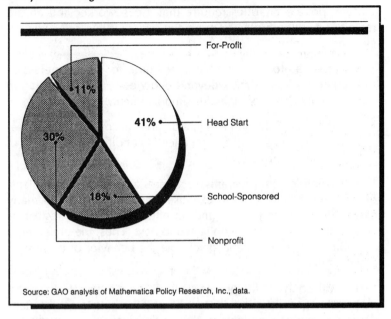

For-Profit

41% — Head Start

School-Sponsored

Nonprofit

Source: GAO analysis of Mathematica Policy Research, Inc., data.

THE NATURE OF CHARITY: ENTITLEMENTS VS. GIFTS

Entitlement programs for welfare are structured so that benefits are granted solely on the basis of personal circumstances. Applicants do not have to give the reasons for their circumstances or explain how they plan to change them in the future. They don't even have to show a willingness to change. In the AFDC program, for example, the requirements for eligibility essentially amount to: (1) low income, (2) very few assets, (3) dependent children and (4) no man in the household. Anyone satisfying these requirements is entitled to benefits. And the word entitlement means "right" — benefits cannot be withdrawn simply because recipients refuse to modify their behavior.

The philosophy of the private sector is quite different. The best private charities do not view the giving of assistance as a "duty" or the receipt of assistance as a "right." Instead, they view charitable assistance as a tool recipients can use intelligently, not only to gain relief but also to change behavior. For example, at many private charities the level of assistance varies considerably from individual to individual. Private agencies usually reserve the right to reduce assistance or withdraw it altogether if recipients do not make behavioral changes.

159

Many private charities require that a caseworker and an aid recipient develop a plan to move the recipient into self-sufficiency. For example:

- At Jessie's House, a transitional home for the homeless in Hampton, Mass., shelter beyond one week is contingent upon positive evidence of individual improvement.

- At the Dallas Salvation Army, aid varies according to the caseworker's evaluation of the recipient's condition and record of behavioral improvement.

Under entitlement programs, recipients and potential recipients of aid have full freedom to exercise their preferences. In many cases, they choose poverty and, in effect, present the rest of us with a welfare bill we are obligated to pay. Thus, the preferences of public welfare recipients determine the behavior of those who pay the bills.

The philosophy of the private sector is quite different. In general, private agencies allow those who pay the bills to set the standards and expect recipients to change their behavior accordingly. In other words, recipients or private sector welfare must adjust their behavior to the preferences of the rest of society, not the other way around.

If we accept the view that individuals should take responsibility for supporting themselves and their families and that welfare assistance should be administered in a way that encourages this behavior, it follows that the approach of our best private charities is far superior to that of entitlement programs. Because individuals and individual circumstances differ, it is only through hands-on management that we can give relief without encouraging anti-social behavior.

Hands-on management includes the tailoring of aid to individual needs and individual circumstances. Such support, counseling and follow-up is virtually unheard of in federal welfare programs. Indeed, when public welfare recipients request counseling, they frequently are referred to private sector agencies.

GETTING AID TO THOSE WHO NEED IT MOST

A basic premise of the American system is that government is the last resort. In other words, the role of government is to do those socially desirable things that the private sector either will not or cannot do. Ironically, in the field of social welfare this premise has been turned on its head. In the early years of the War on Poverty, federal welfare programs were a social safety net — to provide services the private sector, for one reason or another, did not. Now, it is obvious that just the opposite is true — increasingly, the private sector is reaching people whom government does not reach and offering essential services that government welfare programs do not provide.

TEMPORARY VS. LONG-TERM RELIEF

A prevalent philosophy in the private sector is that most people are fully capable of taking responsibility for their lives in the long term, but that emergencies and crises occur for which help is both necessary and desirable. As a consequence, private sector agencies make it surprisingly easy for recipients to obtain emergency relief. It really is true that, in America, almost anybody can get a free lunch.

That near-universal characteristic of private sector charity is that it's easy to get, but hard to keep. Most government programs, by contrast, have the opposite characteristic: it's hard to get on welfare, but easy to stay there. In the public sector, there are often long waiting times between applying for assistance and receiving aid. One study reported that:

- In Texas, the waiting period is typically two to three weeks for food stamps.

- For AFDC, the waiting period is typically a month after an applicant completes the complicated and cumbersome application forms.

- The Dallas Salvation Army has had to hire a special staff to decipher public welfare regulations and forms so they can refer people who come to them to the proper public agencies.

Once accepted into the public welfare system, however, people find it relatively easy to stay there for a long time:

- Of all women who receive welfare in any given year, about 60 percent receive welfare the next year.

MINIMIZING THE COST OF GIVING

There is considerable evidence that private sector charity makes far more efficient use of resources than do public welfare programs. Although temporary relief in the form of food or shelter is fairly easy to obtain from private agencies, long-term assistance or assistance in the form of cash is far more difficult. For example:

- Before the Dallas Salvation Army will provide cash to help people defray the cost of rent, recipients must present a court-ordered eviction notice showing failure to pay rent.

- Similarly, before that charity will give financial aid to defray the costs of utilities, the recipient must present a notice of termination of service for failure to pay utility bills.

Even when there is evidence of need, good private charities often seek to determine whether the potential recipient has access to other, untapped sources of assistance. For example:

- Before the Dallas Salvation Army will provide continuing assistance to an individual, a caseworker informs the family — including in-laws — and requests assistance from them first.

- The caseworker also makes sure the individual applies for all other public and private aid for which he or she is eligible.

Private sector agencies appear to be much more adept at avoiding unnecessary spending that does not benefit the truly needy and at keeping program costs down by utilizing volunteer labor and donated goods. Private sector charitable activities are diverse and widespread in cities and counties throughout the country. Our knowledge of these activities is skimpy. However, as more research is done the evidence mounts that in area after area the private sector outperforms government.

PRIVATE CHARITY VS. PUBLIC WELFARE: THE COUNTERPOINT

Rabbi David Saperstein

Rabbi David Saperstein is the Director of the Religious Action Center of Reform Judaism, American Reform Jewry's Washington office, representing 1.5 million Reform Jews in 850 synagogues throughout the nation.

In congressional testimony below, he spoke on behalf of much of the organized Jewish community, formally representing the Reform Jewish Movement through the Union of American Hebrew Congregations; the Central Conference of American Rabbis; the Conservative Jewish Movement through the United Synagogue of America; the Reconstructionist Movement through the Federation of Reconstructionist Congregations and Havurot; the National Jewish Community Relations Advisory Council (NJCRAC), the planning and coordinating body for the organized Jewish community, representing a unique partnership of 117 local and 13 national agencies throughout the United States; and, of key importance to the deliberations of this committee, the Council of Jewish Federations, a network of Jewish fundraising and social service delivery agencies that spend several billion dollars each year to provide direct community services to millions of people nation-wide, mostly non-Jews.

■ POINTS TO CONSIDER

1. Discuss the author's beliefs concerning government's and society's roles in aiding the needy.

2. Does his statement support the idea of private charity replacing federal welfare programs? Why or why not?

3. Summarize the author's views on the controversial "Contract with America" welfare reform proposals.

4. Evaluate his stance on the "entitlement" status of welfare benefits.

Excerpted from the testimony of Rabbi David Saperstein, before the Subcommittee on Human Resources of the House Ways and Means Committee, January 30, 1995.

Judaism teaches that helping fellow human beings in need ("tzedaka") is a matter of responsibility, righteousness, and justice — not an act of charity. Such a responsibility rests on both individuals and government.

I am deeply pleased to have the opportunity to speak about the topic of welfare reform, a social, ethical and political issue that cuts to the heart of this nation's values as exemplified through its attitudes toward the poor. Above all, I come to say that no matter how proud we are of the quality and quantity of our programs, how confident we are about the generosity of our constituents, those who suggest that the private charity sector can fill the void of a government withdrawal from guaranteeing assistance for the poor gravely misread the realities that we face. Indeed, such a withdrawal will cripple our ability to maintain current levels of services let alone expand to meet an explosion of new needs.

DEFINING CHARITY

The Jewish tradition offers important perspectives to our current debate over how best to provide for those in need. America's concern for the poor is based, in part, on the legacy of the Jewish ethics derived originally from the Hebrew Bible. Judaism teaches that poverty is destructive of human dignity and that helping fellow human beings in need ("tzedaka") is a matter of responsibility, righteousness, and justice — not an act of charity. Such a responsibility rests on both individuals and government.

The American Jewish community has preserved this legacy by adhering to the dictate, "There shall be no needy among you" (Deuteronomy, 15:4). We have sought to implement these ideals by working to ameliorate the plight of the poor, the disenfranchised, the elderly, the sick, and the young. The Jewish community puts these ethics into practice every day through our Federation network of social service activities and the charitable activities of our synagogues.

In almost every area of social welfare concerns, the Jewish tradition mandated that it was not only the right, but the obligation of the society and the public sphere to intervene in the economic and social institutions of our society to make them fairer and more equitable. In the Talmudic period, beginning nearly 2,000 years ago, the Jewish community supplemented the obligations of private charity with an elaborate system of public welfare — the first recorded in history — including food, money, burial and clothing funds as well as publicly funded schools for rich and poor alike.

By the Middle Ages, these had grown into a widespread network of social welfare institutions for the poor, including a broad array of food programs, health care funds, dowry funds, funds to rescue and absorb refugees, shelter and food for poor travelers, and education programs. Since members of the Jewish community were compelled to support these institutions, they are analogous in our time to the institutions of government and not the voluntary private charities.

Underlying these programs was a pervasive concern for the inherent value and equality of each person leading to the requirement that, whenever possible, help must be given to the needy in such a way as to enhance the dignity of the recipient. For example, those who claimed that they were poor were given relief immediately and investigation of the claim was done afterwards. Now, the Rabbis knew that some freeloaders would sneak into such a system, but with a sense of frustration and irony, the Talmud found a use even for the freeloaders, noting, "Be good to the impostors. Without them our stinginess would lack its chief excuse." More importantly, since tzedaka is an individual as well as a communal obligation, the communal authorities taxed every person in the community. Even the poor who were the recipients of welfare funds were taxed. This helped each person fulfill the *mitzvah* (commandment) of tzedaka and prevented the stratification of society into two classes. Every person was a giver. Each person — even the poor — helped the poor. But no requirement more enhanced the dignity of the poor than the understanding of our tradition (and, I am confident, that of this committee), that the highest form of charity, was, in the words of Rabbi Moses ben Maimon (Maimonides), the greatest of the Medieval Jewish scholars, to avoid charity by providing a loan or a job.

GOVERNMENT SUPPORT

Today, we continue to believe that the larger community must play a central role in providing for the poor in ways that enable them to live independently, with dignity, and to move from poverty to economic self-sufficiency. In a speech before the Government Affairs Institute at the 1994 Council of Jewish Federations General Assembly, the President of the Jewish Federation of Metropolitan Chicago, Steven B. Nasatir, described the activities of the Federation Social Services in Chicago. He states that, in Chicago alone: "Despite our comprehensive network, we cannot provide the ongoing income maintenance and child care services required by poor families, or those who are elderly or disabled. We cannot be the safety net, as much as we might want to be. We raised and are spending $27 million [not including service fees and other supplemental fund raising done by our agencies] for local services in Chicago this year. We also spend another $23 million in government funds under various contracts we and our agencies have. These numbers do not include yet another $68 million in government funds, including Medicaid, which support our Mt. Sinai Hospital Medical Center, 80 percent of whose revenues come from government-funded programs enabling them to serve the West Side of Chicago."

"The point is that if there is any diminution of government support for the $23 million worth of social services and employment and training programs, the Jewish community of Chicago will not be able to make up the difference. We struggle mightily to maintain our local fund raising campaign and to produce some increased giving each year. If government-funded programs are cut, then the vulnerable people we now serve will just not be served."

Marvin Olasky (author of *The Tragedy of American Compassion*), an influential writer on these issues who has helped shape the current debate, argues that individual "churches, synagogues, and mosques" will step up and increase their programs to fill the void of government's withdrawal from welfare. Clearly, however, Central Synagogue's resources are over-burdened and its facilities are over-crowded, as are the resources of all synagogues, Federations, and community centers across the country. It is not only unfair, but more importantly unrealistic to expect such private charity organizations to provide the services that are currently administered by the government.

Across the nation, programs have already stretched their resources to meet the needs of those in their communities. These institutions would not be able to provide even basic services if government programs are further cut back. The states, already pressed for funds, are highly unlikely to make up the difference. Repeated studies of the non-profit sector generally and the religious community specifically refute the notion that they can provide for the truly needy without an expanded partnership with government. This committee must not ignore this data in deciding how to reform welfare.

As Diana Aviv, Director of the Washington Action Office of the Council of Jewish Federations, stated in written testimony before this subcommittee:

"I believe that it is unrealistic to think that billions of additional dollars will pour into charitable coffers if the public sector retreats from providing basic income support to people in this country. The Jewish Federation network is one of the finest social service systems in the country. Our collective campaigns raised nearly $1 billion in 1994. But in 1995, we are struggling to keep our campaigns at last year's level, and in some economically hard hit communities we are failing. We will do our best to restore our system to vigorous health, and I suspect that we and other charitable institutions will succeed in doing better. But it is imperative that the federal government maintain its role in the public-private partnership that has been created for caring for our nation's needy."

TODAY'S WELFARE DEBATE

The Jewish organizations I represent are especially concerned about provisions that would have the following effects: taking a federal safety net away from poor children; defunding and devaluing AFDC and food nutrition programs from entitlement status; arbitrarily ending benefits to women without providing employment options; and penalizing legal immigrants. Many provisions in the Personal Responsibility Act, the Contract with America's welfare bill, would produce these undesirable ends. Even beyond this specific legislation, a variety of suggested reform proposals include some or all of these harmful elements.

IMPACT ON CHILDREN

The ultimate judgment of a nation — of its values, its honor, its basic decency — rests upon how it treats its children. A nation that neglects its children, that allows children to go hungry or homeless, that fails adequately to educate its children, is a nation that short-changes its future.

In the zeal to reform the welfare system, members of Congress must not forget how the actions they are now considering affect our children and America's future. America already has too many homeless children huddled and shivering against winter's chill without adequate shelter, too many children whose young stomachs know too well the empty pain of hunger. Those who would alter the welfare system in order to cut budgets will cite the financial benefits of their cuts, will claim that by reducing the national deficit they are securing our future. But by reducing that deficit and penalizing children — by making the weakest and neediest among us bear the burden of reform — they only bleaken that future.

There are four ways that the Personal Responsibility Act and other bills would devastate millions of American children. First, these proposals would permanently bar children from receiving AFDC benefits if their mothers were unmarried and under the age of eighteen. Second, they would disqualify children who were conceived while their mothers were already receiving AFDC. Third, they would prohibit children from receiving AFDC benefits if paternity had not been established. Finally, one of the most controversial provisions would favor state guardianship of children over familial care by allowing states to spend funds, saved from the paternity exclusion, on orphanages and group homes for teen mothers.

The Center on Budget and Policy Priorities estimates that if these proposals were in full force today, at least five million children, more than half of the AFDC caseload, would lose all cash assistance. The paternity requirement alone would immediately

168

end assistance to 2.8 million children — 29 percent of all children now receiving AFDC.

BLOCK GRANTS FOR AFDC AND FOOD PROGRAMS

Many legislators now champion proposals to block-grant AFDC, food stamps, and other federal nutrition programs. They argue that block grants would provide states with more flexibility in administering assistance to their own populations. In reality, block-granting AFDC would devalue the program from its current status as an entitlement program with guaranteed full funding. Instead, the program would fall within the discretionary fund subject to budgetary caps, the annual appropriations process, and incomplete funding. Funding for vital programs like child care and child support would be capped and forced to compete for funds with other deserving programs for scarce federal dollars. And, given the current push by many legislators for a Balanced Budget Amendment to the U.S. Constitution, AFDC would be among the discretionary funds most vulnerable to cuts or total elimination.

Similar proposals would combine food stamps with other nutrition programs, such as the school lunch and breakfast program and WIC, and would turn them over to the states in the form of block grants. These are among some of the nation's most successful and cost-effective programs representing a wise investment in our children and our future. Like the change in the status of AFDC, block-granting the food stamp program, the most critical safety net for poor families, would lead to reduction in funding, increased competition among programs, and, potentially, total elimination.

The Center on Budget and Policy Priorities estimates that if the Congress follows this approach and turns these programs over to the states in the form of block grants, the total cuts in federal funding for food, housing and income programs would reach approximately $57 billion over four years. Nobody can articulate the social costs of undercutting the poor.

ARBITRARY TIME LIMITS AND EMPLOYMENT

Many legislators now support proposals to cut women and their children off of AFDC after two years. New proposals would allow states to cut off all of a family's AFDC benefits, without assuring that the recipient has reasonable access to work, whether it be in the private sector or subsidized by the federal government. The Jewish groups I represent have grave concerns about this approach to welfare reform not only for powerful moral reasons, but practical reasons as well. Where do supporters of these time limits suggest that families without incomes live? Where will their meals come from? How will they clothe and support their children? Time limits can be part of an overall reform program but not in the form of imposing a lifetime limit on any form of assistance without regard to availability of training, jobs, necessary social support and other impediments to work. Such proposals cannot possibly meet the varied and complex needs of all AFDC recipients.

PRIVATIZING THE WELFARE STATE: POINT AND COUNTERPOINT

Jeffrey Tucker vs. National Religious Organizations

The following point and counterpoint examine proposals to lessen government involvement in aiding the poor — privatizing the welfare state. The first piece was written by Jeffrey Tucker for the Free Market, *the newsletter of the Ludwig Von Mises Institute in Auburn, Alabama. The counterpoint is a statement of shared principles on welfare reform by National Religious Organizations and Leaders.*

■ **POINTS TO CONSIDER**

1. Why is Tucker dissatisfied with both government's and private organizations' welfare and social spending?

2. Discuss the author's proposal for welfare reform.

3. Summarize the reasons why many national religious organizations and leaders are dissatisfied with Republican welfare reform proposals.

4. How do the national religious organizations and leaders feel about the role of government in welfare?

5. Compare and contrast the two views about government and welfare. How do you feel about the issue?

Jeffrey Tucker, "Privatize the Welfare State?" **Free Market,** January, 1995: 5-6, and "A Statement of Shared Principles on Welfare Reform by National Religious Organizations," April, 1995.

The phrase "End Welfare as We Know It" is a classic Clinton evasion. It sounds bold and "neo-liberal" at first, but on close examination it collapses into nothingness. Almost any change in a policy qualifies by ending it "as we know it." It could mean more spending and retribution.

In either case, the bill-writing, policy-proposing industry is overjoyed that "welfare reform" will bring another boon year along the lines of "health-care reform." In short order, the public will be asked to root for one of hundreds of treatises promising to turn South Central L.A. into Malibu. Judging from the initial offerings, none of these bills will result in cuts to overall government spending.

On the plus side, Clinton's phrase did conjure up, however vaguely, the prospect of getting rid of the welfare state, which, depending on how "welfare" is defined, consists of between one-third and four-fifths of the budget. Suddenly, what was once advocated only by "extremists" Ludwig von Mises, Henry Hazlitt, and Murray Rothbard has become, if not respectable, at least not unthinkable.

Is the ultimate solution to "privatize the welfare state," to use the newest phrase being batted around the land of policy wonks? As with Clinton's famous words, the term "privatize" means different things to different people. To HUD official Andrew "Mario's Son" Cuomo, it means turning over federal housing monies to private non-profit organizations. As the founder and former administrator of a government-funded homeless shelter in New York City, he discovered this to be a more profitable way to pursue Left-wing policies than the old-fashioned public-sector approach.

Part of the glory of the private sector — profit or non-profit — is its financial accountability. But give a privately-owned entity a government grant, and that virtue comes to an end. Andrew Cuomo himself demonstrated this by building publicly-funded projects for "the poor" in ritzy suburban areas, thereby driving down everyone else's property values.

The proposal to "privatize the welfare state" isn't limited to the Left. An idea bandied about the Right suggests that individual income-tax filers name their favorite charities on their tax forms. Up to 20% of the taxes they pay will go directly from the U.S.

Treasury to the selected non-profits' bank accounts. It's a souped-up plan to spread government subsidies more widely.

About 60% of the non-profit sector's resources already come from the government. As Thomas DiLorenzo and James Bennett have documented, much of this money is used to lobby for more government spending, which in turn is allocated back to the non-profits. Proposals from the Left and the Right to "privatize" in this manner would only make this scandalous practice worse.

When non-profit organizations accept government money, they compromise their independence. Many are already little more than lobbyists and grafters, virtual adjuncts of labor unions, welfare clients, and the subsidized corporate establishment. It is especially perverse for non-profits pushing free enterprise to receive funding from the government's pipeline. The few who refused such funds on principle would be at a distinct disadvantage to those living off the taxpayer.

The correct word for this approach is not "privatizing" but "contracting out," that is, to have the private sector do efficiently what the government is doing inefficiently. But why should we want to do that? Government waste and inefficiency is troubling, but, even so, it is often a saving grace. If government worked as well as the private sector, we would be doomed. Who needs bad law enforced with new vigor, or bad programs better run?

Real privatization of the welfare state requires more. It requires returning property to its original owners, or at least the cessation of further redistribution. A dollar in private capital can do more work, and do it better, than a hundred taken by the government and redistributed. Doing this doesn't require complex "reforms," a thousand pages long. It takes persistent efforts to cut spending and taxes, a solution that is somehow beyond the grasp of Washington's bipartisan planners.

National Religious Organizations: The Counterpoint

As people of faith and religious commitment, we are called to stand with and seek justice for people who are poor. Central to our religious traditions, sacred texts, and teachings is a divine mandate to side with and protect the poor. We share a conviction, therefore, that welfare reform must not focus on eliminating programs but on eliminating poverty and the damage it inflicts on children (who are 2/3 of all welfare recipients), on their parents, and on the rest of society.

We recognize the benefit to the entire community of helping people move from welfare into the job market when possible and appropriate. We fear, however, that reform will fail if it ignores labor market issues such as unemployment and an inadequate minimum wage and important family issues such as the affordability of child care and the economic value of care-giving in the home. Successful welfare reform will depend on addressing these concerns as well as a whole range of such related issues as pay equity, affordable housing, and the access to health care.

We believe that people are more important than the sum of their economic activities. Successful welfare reform demands more than economic incentives and disincentives. It depends on overcoming both biased assumptions about race, gender and class that feed hostile social stereotypes about people living in poverty and suspicions that people with perspectives other than our own are either indifferent or insincere. Successful welfare reform will depend ultimately upon finding not only a common ground of policies but a common spirit about the need to pursue them for all.

The following principles do not exhaust our concerns or resolve all issues raised. The principles will serve nonetheless as our guide in assessing proposed legislation in the national welfare debate. We hope they may also serve as a rallying point for a common effort with others throughout the nation.

An acceptable welfare program must result in lifting people out of poverty, not merely in reducing welfare rolls.

- The federal government should define minimum benefit levels of programs serving low-income people below which states will not be permitted to fall. These benefits must be adequate to provide a decent standard of living.

- Welfare reform efforts designed to move people into the work force must create jobs that pay a livable wage and do not displace present workers. Programs should eliminate barriers to employment and provide training and education necessary for inexperienced and young workers to get and hold jobs. Such programs must provide child care, transportation, and other ancillary services that will make participation both possible and

174

WORKFARE NO BETTER THAN WELFARE

The problem, then, is not forcing taxpayers to subsidize idleness, but forcing them to subsidize an unproductive life. Forcing taxpayers to subsidize employers or to provide busy-work for unproductive "jobs" is worse than keeping welfare recipients idle. There is no point to activity or work unless it is productive, and enacting a taxpayer subsidy is a sure way to keep the welfarees unproductive. Subsidizing the idle is immoral and counterproductive; paying people to work and creating jobs for them is also crazy, as well as being more expensive.

Murray Rothbard, "Welfare as We Don't Know It," **Free Market**, April, 1994: 8.

reasonable. If the government becomes the employer of last resort, the jobs provided must pay a family-sustaining wage.

• Disincentives to work should be removed by allowing welfare recipients to retain a larger portion of wage earnings and assets before losing cash, housing, health, child care or other benefits.

• Work-based programs must not impose arbitrary time limits. If mandated, limits must not be imposed without availability of viable jobs at a family-sustaining wage. Even then, some benefit recipients cannot work or should not be required to work. Exemptions should be offered for people with serious physical or mental illness, disabling conditions, responsibilities as caregivers for incapacitated family members, and for those primary caregivers who have responsibility for young children.

• Welfare reform should result in a program that brings together and simplifies the many efforts of federal, state and municipal governments to assist persons and families in need. "One-stop shopping centers" should provide information, counseling, and legal assistance regarding such issues as child support, job training and placement, medical care, affordable housing, food programs and education.

• Welfare reform should acknowledge the responsibility of both government and parents in seeking the well-being of children. No child should be excluded from receiving benefits available to other siblings because of having been born while the mother was on welfare. No child should be completely removed from the safety net because of a parent's failure to fulfill agreements with the government. Increased efforts should also be made to collect a proper level of child support assistance from non-custodial parents.

- Programs designed to replace current welfare programs must be adequately funded. It must be recognized and accepted that these programs will cost more in the short-term than the present Aid to Families with Dependent Children program. However, if welfare reform programs are successfully implemented, they will cost less as the number of families in need of assistance diminishes over the long-term. In financing this effort, funding should not be taken from other programs that successfully serve the poor.

NATIONAL ENDORSING ORGANIZATIONS

Adrian Dominican Sisters
American Baptist Churches, USA
American Ethical Union, Inc., National Leaders Council (AEU)
American Friends Service Committee
Bread for the World
Church of the Brethren, Washington Office
Church Women United
Columban Fathers Justice and Peace Office
Episcopal Church
General Board of Global Ministries of the UMC, Institutional Ministries
General Board of Church and Society, United Methodist Church
Interfaith IMPACT for Justice and Peace
Jesuit Social Ministries, National Office
Evangelical Lutheran Church in America
Maryknoll Society Justice and Peace Office
Mennonite Central Committee, Washington Office
Moravian Church, Northern Province
National Council of Churches
National Council of Jewish Women
NETWORK, A National Catholic Social Justice Lobby
Presbyterian Church (USA), Washington Office
Union of American Hebrew Congregations
Unitarian Universalist Service Committee
United Church of Christ, Office for Church in Society
For Information: Contact National Council of Churches (202) 544-2350

176

BIBLIOGRAPHY

Periodical References

Bidinotto, Robert James. "Cultural Pollution," **The Freeman**. Mar. 1995: 165.

"Bishops Say Welfare Cuts Go Too Far," **Star Tribune**. 19 Mar. 1995: 1A.

Blackburn, Thomas E. "The Welfare Debate as Challenge to the Churches," **National Catholic Reporter**. 6 Jan. 1995: 13.

"Facing Welfare Reform," **America**. 28 Jan. 1995: 3.

Fund, John. "Welfare: Putting People First," **Wall Street Journal**. 14 June 1994: A14.

Gallman, Vanessa. "Welfare Reform Depends on Debunking Myths," **Pioneer Press**. 18 Dec. 1994: 1A.

"Gingrich: Religion-Based Programs Better for Poor," **Human Events**. 13 Jan. 1995.

Glass, Stephen. "Happy Meals, When Lunch Subsidies Are Cut, Kids Eat Better," **Policy Review**. Summer 1995.

Gordon, Linda. "Welfare Reform: A History Lesson," **Dissent**. Summer 1994: 323.

"Governor Tommy Thompson Shows Way on Welfare," **Human Events**. 7 Apr. 1995.

Katz, Jeffrey L. "House Passes Welfare Bill, Senate Likely to Alter It," **Congressional Quarterly Weekly Report**. 25 Mar. 1995.

"Legal Immigration Denied Aid Under House Welfare Reform Bill," **Stewardship of Public Life**. 2nd Quarter 1995: 1.

Levin, Michael. "The Real Reason Welfare Should End," **The Freeman**. Feb. 1995: 111.

Lovern, Beth. "Confessions of a Welfare Mom," **Utne Reader**. July/Aug. 1994: 81.

McGrady, Mary Rose. "Welfare Reform: The View from Covenant House," **America**. 24 Sept. 1994: 7.

Mellor, William H., III. "A Right to Welfare?" **Reason**. Oct. 1994: 67.

Mercier, Rick. "Welfare Reform," **Z Magazine**. Sept. 1994: 26.

Nader Ralph. "Big Government's Double Standard," **Liberal Opinion Week**. 30 Jan. 1995: 5.

Nader, Ralph. "Corporate Welfare," **Multinational Monitor**. Jan./Feb. 1993: 42.

Nelson, Lars-Erik. "Ending Corporate Welfare Would Benefit Everyone," **Liberal Opinion Week**. 20 Mar. 1995.

Olasky, Marvin. "A Welfare Fantasy," **The American Enterprise**. Jan./Feb. 1994.

Page,Clarence. "Poverty Is Not Just a Black Problem," **Liberal Opinion Week**. 13 Mar. 1995: 9.

Polakow, Valene. "A Tightrope Without a Net," **The Nation**. 1 May 1995: 590.

Rachleff, Peter. "The Dream Fades for Ordinary Americans," **Star Tribune**. 6 Feb. 1995: 3D.

Reed, Lawrence W. "The Right Direction for Welfare Reform," **The Freeman**. May 1995: 294.

Rosen, Ruth. "Their Welfare and Ours," **Tikkun**. Vol. 10, no. 1: 75.

Ross, Grace. "End Poverty as We Know It, Not Welfare," **Resist**. May/June 1994: 1.

Safire, William. "On Ending Welfare as We Know It," **Star Tribune**. 13 July 1995.

Schaper, Donna E. "What Can We Do for Ourselves?" **Christian Social Action**. Mar. 1995: 12.

"Sex, Families, Race, Poverty, Welfare," **The American Enterprise**. Jan./Feb. 1995: 33.

"Should U.S. Taxpayers Subsidize Illegitimacy?" **Human Events**. 31 Mar. 1995: 1.

Snow, Tony. "Clinton Broadens Gap Between Rich and Poor," **Conservative Chronicle**. 2 Nov. 1994: 5.

Snow, Tony. "Republicans Should Focus on Killing Corporate Welfare," **Pioneer Press**. 10 Mar. 1995: 9A

Warren, Carol. "Welfare Reform More Complicated in Real Life," **National Catholic Reporter**. 31 Mar. 1995: 28.

Weaver, Carolyn L. "Welfare Payments to the Disabled: Making America Sick?" **The American Enterprise**. Jan./Feb. 1994.

"Welfare Can't Be Reformed, Must Be Ended, Study Says," **Cato Policy Report.**

"Welfare Reform: Implications of Proposals on Legal Immigrants' Benefits," **Government Accounting Office Report**. Feb. 1995.

Wisz, Gerald. "Ending Welfare as They Knew It," **The Freeman**. Oct. 1994: 540.

Book References

Achinstein, Asher. **The Welfare State: The Case for and Against.** Washington, D.C.: Legislative Reference Service, 1950.

Barr, Nicholas. **The Economics of the Welfare State.** Palo Alto: Stanford University Press, 1987.

Baumol, William J. **Welfare Economics and the Theory of the State.** Cambridge: Harvard University Press, 1967.

Bennet, James T. and Thomas J. DiLorenzo. **Unhealthy Charities.** New York: Basic Books, 1994.

Bergson, Abram. **Essays in Normative Economics.** Cambridge: Harvard University Press, 1966.

Blin, J.M. **Patterns and Configurations in Economic Science.** Boston: D. Reidel Publishing, 1973.

Campbell, Donald E. **Resource Allocation Mechanisms.** Cambridge University Press, 1987.

Carter, Charles F. **Wealth: An Essay on the Purpose of Economics.** Basic Books, 1969.

Current Issues in the Economics of Welfare. ed. Nicholas Barr and David Whynes. New York: St. Martin's Press, 1993.

Dasgupta, Ajit Kumar. **Cost-benefit Analysis: Theory and Practice**. London: MacMillan, 1972.

Dasgupta, Ajit Kumar. **Growth, Development and Welfare**. Blackwell, 1988.

Davidson, Alexander. **Two Models of Welfare: The Origins and Development of the Welfare State in Sweden and New Zealand**. Acta Universitatis Upsaliensis, 1989.

Dobb, Maurice Herbert. **Welfare Economics and the Economics of Socialism: Towards a Commonsense Critique**. Cambridge University Press, 1969.

Esping-Andersen, Gosta. **The Three Worlds of Welfare Capitalism**. Princeton: Princeton University Press, 1990.

Feldman, Allan. **Welfare Economics and Social Theory**. Boston: Martinus Nijhoff Publishing, 1980.

Gordon, Linda. **Pitied But Not Entitled: Single Mothers and the History of Welfare**. Free Press, 1994.

Gordon, Scott. **Welfare, Justice, and Freedom**. New York: Columbia University Press, 1980.

Hahnel, Robin. **Quiet Revolution in Welfare Economics**. Princeton: Princeton University Press, 1990.

Hamlin, Alan P. **Ethics, Economics and the State**. New York: St. Martin's Press, 1986.

Harberger, Arnold C. **Taxation and Welfare**. Boston: Little, Brown, 1974.

Hazlitt, Henry. **The Conquest of Poverty**. New Rochelle, NY: ArlingtonHouse, 1973.

Hyman, David N. **The Economics of Governmental Activity**. New York: Holt, Rinehart and Winston,1973.

Johansson, Per-Olav. **An Introduction to Modern Welfare Economics**. Cambridge: Cambridge University Press, 1991.

Land, Philip S., SJ. **Shaping Welfare Consensus: U.S. Catholic Bishops' Contribution**. Center for Concern, 1994.

LaPatra, Jack W. **Public Welfare Systems**. Springfield, IL: Thomas, 1976.

Melnick, R. Shep. **Between the Lines: Interpreting Welfare Rights**. Washington, D.C.: The Brookings Institution, 1994.

Mishan, Edward J. **Economic Efficiency and Social Welfare: Selected Essays on Fundamental Aspects of the Economic Theory of Social Welfare**. Boston: George Allen & Unwin, 1981.

Mishra, Ramesh. **The Welfare State in Capitalist Society: Policies of Retrenchment and Maintenance in Europe, North America and Australia**. Toronto: Toronto University Press, 1990.

Mueller, Dennis C. **Public Choice II**. Cambridge: Cambridge University Press, 1989.

Musolf, Lloyd D. **Government and the Economy: Promoting the General Welfare**. Scott, Foresman, 1967.

Olasky, Marvin. **The Tragedy of American Compassion**. Washington, D.C.: Regnery Publishing, Inc., 1992.

Pettit, Philip. **Judging Justice: An Introduction to Contemporary Political Philosophy**. Boston: Routledge and Kegan Paul, 1980.

Rowley, Charles Kershaw. **Welfare Economics: A Liberal Restatement**. New York: Wiley, 1975.

Sen, Amartya Kumar. **Inequality Reexamined**. Cambridge: Harvard University Press, 1992.

Sklar, Holly. **Chaos or Community: Seeking Solutions , Not Scapegoats to Bad Economics**. Boston: South End Press, 1995.

Smith, Edmund Arthur. **Social Welfare: Principles and Concepts**. New York: Association Press, 1965.

Tullock, Gordon. **Private Wants, Public Means: An Economic Analysis of the Desirable Scope of Government**. Basic Books, 1970.

Usher, Dan. **The Collected Papers of Dan Usher**. Brookfield, VT: Elgar, 1994.

Whitcomb, David K. **Externalities and Welfare**. New York: Columbia University Press, 1972.

Williams, Walter. **Outrageous Injustice of the Welfare State**. Recorded in Washington, D.C.: Laissez Faire, 1993.

INDEX